Stories

STIRLING AND ROB ROY COUNTRY

Rennie McOwan
Sir Walter Scott
and
John Mackay

Lang**Syne**

PUBLISHING

WRITING *to* REMEMBER

Lang**Syne**

PUBLISHING

WRITING *to* REMEMBER

Strathclyde Business Centre
120 Carstairs Street, Glasgow G40 4JD
Tel: 0141 554 9944 Fax: 0141 554 9955
E-mail: scottishmemories@aol.com
www.scottish-memories.co.uk

Printed by JSB Print, Glasgow
Design and artwork by Roy Boyd and David Braysher
© Lang Syne Publishers Ltd 2003
ISBN 1-85217-106-5

contents

Introduction

For over 800 years, in war and peace, the castle at Stirling has occupied centre stage in our nation's story. Situated atop a 250ft rock, it dominates a strategic crossing point of the River Forth and, as the old Scots saying goes, *whoever held Stirling, held Scotland.*

William Wallace recaptured the castle from the English after the Battle of Stirling Bridge in 1297, but seven years later it fell to King Edward I, the notorious Hammer of the Scots. A decade was to pass before Robert the Bruce won the castle back in 1314, after crushing the auld enemy at Bannockburn.

In these pages we tell the story of the battles and of key events that shaped the castle's story as it became the favourite residence of Scotland's kings and queens.

We then move downtown to recall grim times in the old jail where the hangman ruled the roost (more fortunate victims got off with a public whipping through the streets). We find out about about the vile trade of body-snatchers, a glowing hand with magical powers and the wolf that saved Stirling from destruction.

The town dates back to 1000 A.D. An early charter, granted by Alexander II in 1226, was addressed to a long established community of merchants and craftsmen. Spellings through the ages have varied from Stryvelling to Strivilin and some claim the derivation to be from the word 'stife' - a most appropriate signification.

Next we journey to Loch Lomond for the story of Scotland's most famous and beautiful loch - it has waves without wind, fish without fins and islands that float! Ever present are clan feuds, cattle rustlers and even pirates! Discover the secrets of the beautiful Trossachs and marvel at the adventures of its most infamous son - Rob Roy McGregor. We learn how a foul deed by a friend drove Rob to become an outlaw whose primary object in life was to plunder those "friendly to the revolutionary Government or that most obnoxious of measures - the union of the kingdoms".

His daring thefts over the years brought him much money and many cattle. He even operated a protection racket! However, most folk liked Rob because he tried to avoid violence and often helped the poor.

Battle of Stirling Bridge

by Rennie McOwan

Stirling Castle looks to two sites in particular that have prominently figured in battles and power-struggles over the years - Stirling Bridge and the Abbey Craig, which is now topped by the Wallace Monument
This great tower and viewpoint was erected as a national monument in 1869 to one of Scotland's greatest heroes.

The old stone bridge of Stirling was dominated by the castle and has many a tale to tell of its own. But it was another nearby bridge of wood on stone foundations which was to be the scene of a bloody battle. No-one is precisely certain where this older bridge stood. Some historians say it was at Kildean, others that it was nearer Cambuskenneth Abbey, but no-one denies it was of great strategic importance and — as happened so often — controlled by whoever held the castle.

When the tide is out and the river level falls the remains of wooden piles can be seen, and if these are the actual foundations they mark a watery grave for many a brave knight and many a hardy footsoldier.

The story begins when nearly all of Scotland was under the conquering armies of Edward I of England. The Earl of Surrey was appointed Guardian of Scotland.

Sir Hugh de Cressingham, a Churchman, was treasurer and ensured all the key castles such as Stirling were garrisoned by his own soldiers.

But not all Scots were prepared to accept English rule. William Wallace was the son of a small landowner, Sir Malcolm Wallace, and he was born at Elderslie, near Paisley. When he grew up he determined to restore control of Scotland to its own people. He was tall and strong, and legends of the time say he had fair hair, piercing eyes and a wound-mark on the left-side of his chin.

Wallace began by brawling with soldiers from the garrisons and then serious fighting broke out as resistance grew. It was said that his wife was slain in Lanark during a struggle for possession of the town.

Legend also tells that the Governor of Ayr invited Scottish nobles and other leaders to a meeting and they were then hanged in twos after they had entered the building. Wallace was invited but was warned in time.

In retaliation, he and his men raided Ayr at night, fastened from the outside the doors of the wooden houses in which the English garrison were billeted and then set them on fire.

More men joined Wallace, and he attacked towns and isolated castles, and gradually began to control much of Scotland. He was not a great
noble, only the son of a minor laird, but his strength, striking appearance,
personality and military skill persuaded men of higher rank to serve under
his command.

The Earl of Surrey began to fear that Wallace would conquer all of
Scotland, and he sent urgent messages to King Edward, asking him to send
a large army to crush Wallace. Over 30,000 knights and footsoldiers were
sent north to Stirling. Wallace heard the news when he was beseiging
Dundee; the only town north of the Tay still in English hands, and he quickly broke off the siege.

He planned to halt the English army at the inevitable strategic point
of Stirling. By forced marches he speedily got his army of 10,000 to Stirling
and took up position on the Abbey Craig, hiding most of his men among the
trees.

He had excellent observation over the lower ground and could see
the English soldiers gathering together on the south side of the river. Wallace
knew that the wooden bridge across the Forth was so narrow that it could
only take columns of men and horses if they marched two abreast. He could
not really believe the English commanders would permit their army to cross,
thus dividing it into two halves, but he hoped against hope that they would.

There was a ford nearby, suitable when the tide was out. The Earl of
Surrey was an experienced soldier and did not want the army to cross over
the bridge and attack the strongly placed Scots, but Cressingham is said to
have contemptuously insisted on speed and to have been certain of victory.

Wallace watched the oncoming horsemen with bated breath and
great satisfaction, and gave instructions to his troops to get ready for instant
action.

A very brave Knight, Sir Marmaduke de Twenge, who was Keeper
of Stirling Castle, led the English heavy cavalry across the bridge, and they
were then followed by other horsemen and footsoldiers of a division commanded by Cressingham.

Because of the narrowness of the bridge the pace was slow. It was
midday before about half of the English army reached the north bank of the
Forth and fanned out in a defensive bridgehead.

Then Wallace struck!

A large group of Scots spearmen made as if to go to the riverbank

Very few survived on the north side of the river

to block the English advance, and then suddenly changed direction. They formed a tight wedge of levelled spears and charged at the portion of the English column just leaving the bridge. They crashed into the ill-prepared soldiers, dislodged them and occupied one end of the bridge.

Then, back to back, fighting fiercely, they held off the hampered English troops on the bridge who could only come at them two at a time, and at the same time they beat off counter-attacks from the troops on the north bank who realised the Scots now had control of the bridge and had cut their army in half. Marmaduke de Twenge refused to follow some of his men who leaped into the waters of the Forth and tried to swim across, and he managed to cut his way back on to the bridge and rejoin his comrades.

But, after that, the Scots kept the bridge-end firmly closed. Wallace, timing his main charge to perfection, sent his army crashing into the English horsemen, driving them back on Cressingham's men.

Surrey and the men of the stranded other half of his army watched in bitter anger as the long spears of the Scots drove both footsoldiers and cavalry back in disorder, until they poured over the river-banks and into the waters of the Forth.

Thousands perished on the banks or were drowned. The Earl of Surrey bravely tried to force his way over the bridge, but was blocked by corpses, wounded men, maimed horses kicking out and screaming, and the on-coming rush of the Scots.

Very few survived on the north side of the river and there was further consternation when part of the bridge collapsed and fell into the water.

Some reports of the time say Wallace had the bridge undermined so that when key pins were driven out it fell into the Forth, but others say the bridge gave way under the weight of the fighting. Whatever the reason, the collapsed bridge helped the Scots who had nearly all of their army on the Abbey Craig side, and it spelled doom for the now-surrounded bridgehead who could not be reinforced.

Cressingham was among the many slain: his corpse had a spear driven through it.

Wallace followed up the carnage by ordering his men to cross at the ford at Kildean and to pursue Surrey's division.

The Earl eventually retreated to Berwick, and returned to England. The remnants of the English army were later attacked by another Scots force at Torwood, stationed by Wallace to be ready for just such an eventuality, and here again casualties were heavy.

The victory was complete.

Ahead of Wallace lay further victories, the freeing of his country, the re-establishment of Scottish trade with the Continent and raids into England. Also ahead of him lay eventual defeat at the Battle of Falkirk, betrayal to King Edward, and a cruel execution in London.

His head was placed on a pole at London Bridge and other parts of his corpse were sent to Newcastle, Berwick, Stirling and Perth as a warning to others.

But the fires that Wallace kindled were not put out and were eventually to burn again under King Robert the Bruce.

The Wallace Monument dominates the area around Stirling, the river which was part of his plan and the ancient castle which he took after his overwhelming victory at Stirling Bridge.

Sir William Wallace

For Scotland's freedom

King Robert the Bruce was very angry. His brother. Sir Edward, had made a pledge that might well ruin all he had planned and struggled for over so many years.

The King of the Scots had been fighting guerilla actions against the English armies in Scotland since he was crowned at Scone in March 1306. His reign had not begun well.

His small army had been quickly defeated and scattered. His friends were hanged, or fled into hiding. His relatives were imprisoned and cruelly treated. His estates were forfeited. But still he had continued the fight, determined to succeed and to restore Scotland's independence.

He spent the winter abroad, returned to Scotland in 1307 and waged unceasing war against the English, and the Scots who supported them and who did not agree with Bruce's claim to be King.

He knew he could not yet win a pitched battle. He did not have enough men or a secure base. But he had outstanding commanders, tested in many a skirmish and ambush, and he made skilful use of the Scottish forests, and of lonely glens and mountains, to hide his small band.

He found isolated garrisons of English soldiers, and the Scots who aided them, and demolished them. He defeated sizeable English forces on ground of his own choosing. He captured strong-points and towns, sacked and burned the buildings, destroyed weapons, food and stores and then melted back into the countryside. It was the classic guerilla-pattern that we have seen so often in modern times, during the Second World War and afterwards.

By keeping rigidly to this pattern, he gradually began to drive the English forces back into the main castles and keeps. Many Scots flocked to join his standard. He totally crushed the powerful Comyn family, who did not want Bruce as king, and he was then free to turn his whole attention to the English forces.

Gradually, the leading Scottish towns and castles fell to him. An exception was Stirling Castle, strong and dominating, controlling all traffic north and south and the narrow waistland of Scotland. It had an unrivalled strategic importance. It was said of Stirling that it was a brooch that clasped Highlands and Lowlands together.

Sir Edward Bruce had laid seige the castle and after three months he had a parley with the castle commander. Sir Philip Mowbray. The commander said he would surrender if an English army failed to appear within three leagues of the castle by Midsummer's Day 1314.

Edward Bruce impetuously agreed, perhaps carried away by the steady flow of Scottish successes. He had always been a man of action, and indeed it was he who had encouraged Bruce to persevere in the struggle when they had re-landed on the Scottish mainland.

When King Robert was told he was deeply displeased. He knew that the pledge meant that the English now had a chance to meet the Scots in pitched battle, an event he had deliberately avoided. Bruce was not sure his men were ready. He knew that the English could put a huge army of armoured knights into the field, and that they could produce many archers who had been the decisive element in other battles.

It was the archers who had defeated Wallace at the Battle of Falkirk in 1298, the hail of arrows breaking the schiltron, the ring, of Scottish spearmen, thus opening up gaps and leaving them prey to the charge of knights on heavy horses.

Bruce's hit-and-hide tactics had been successful. Now the pattern was to change and he was uneasy. But the deed was done, and the pledge had been made.

Stirling Castle, which had proved a stumbling block for many armies, was to be the price for the victor of one of the greatest conflicts of the Scottish Wars of Independence.

King Edward II of England was not the iron-hard soldier his father had been, the famous "Hammer of the Scots", but he was still determined to accept the challenge from this upstart Scot. He was certain that if he could defeat the Scots in pitched battle he could win back all that he had lost in Scotland since Bruce was crowned and either rule himself or install a puppet King.

He gathered a huge army of 25,000 foot soldiers armed with spears, axes and swords. He also recruited many Welsh archers, armed with longbows. He had over 2,000 heavy cavalry, and they were expected to crush the Scots troops in the same way as modern tanks could over-run infantrymen.

King Edward also had the help of some Scots, such as the Comyns, MacDougalls and MacNabs, who opposed Bruce. It was a vast army for the time, with a supply and baggage train of over 200 wagons.

So confident was King Edward and his commanders of an easy victory, that in addition to food, spare arms, equipment and pay for the troops, they carried furniture and other goods for some of the nobles who were to be given Scottish estates once the expected crushing victory had taken place.

But Bruce held many cards. His army, although small, was well disciplined, accustomed to command, lean and experienced, and had been together as a close-knit fighting unit for some years. He had about 7,000 soldiers, but only a few hundred cavalrymen, mounted on light horses. Bruce had two months to bring his army to readiness for a pitched battle.

He obviously had to prevent the relief of Stirling Castle, and he had also to try to destroy King Edward's army.

He was determined not to repeat the mistakes of the battle of Falkirk, and trained his men to become proficient in quickly forming the Scottish battle ring, the schiltron. He also taught them to "break hedgehog" and to counter-attack in formation, a device intended to overcome the problem of immobility shown at Falkirk. His men had 12 foot spears, swords, axes and dirks, protective helmets, mail gloves to hold the spears, and padded coats to stop arrows.

In defence the schiltron formed an unbroken wall of spears against the charge of the armoured knights. In advance, it relied on numbers to add weight and to press home the attack with levelled spears.

Practice and discipline were essential and Bruce saw that his men had these.

He split his force into four divisions, under battle-tried commanders. The first was commanded by Randolph, Earl of Moray, who had captured Edinburgh Castle in a daring raid the year before. The second division was led by Sir Edward Bruce, no doubt pensive about what his rash promise to the commander of the castle had brought. The third was led by the feared Sir James Douglas.

Next to Bruce, Douglas was the greatest hero among the Scots. Because of his dark complexion he was called the "Blacky Douglas". He became such a terror to the invaders that mothers used to repeat a rhyme to their children:

> *'Hush thee, hush thee, do not fret thee,*
> *The Black Douglas will not get thee!'*

It was Douglas who had planned the famous capture of his own castle of Douglasdale, in Lanarkshire. When the English garrison had attended church on Palm Sunday, Douglas' men were in the congregation with weapons below their cloaks. At a signal from Douglas, who dropped his cloak and shouted "A Douglas! A Douglas!" they fell upon the garrison. All were killed. Then they took the castle, replenished their own stores, and made a great heap of casks, foodstuffs, and corpses and set fire to it all. This famous raid was known as the Douglas Larder.

The King commanded the fourth, the strongest division.

Bruce was also aided by about 2,000 "small folk", the ordinary people who had lost homes and families and who wanted to join the fray. They were poorly armed and ill-disciplined, but legend has it that they were to play a key part in the battle.

The cavalry, under Sir Alexander Keith, were to be kept for a special role.

There were men from nearly all parts of Scotland in the King's army, from Ross and Moray, from towns like Inverness, Elgin and Nairn, from areas like Buchan, Mar, Angus, Strathearn, Menteith and Lennox. There were men from central Scotland and from the Borders.

The King's own division had Macdonalds from the west, from Kintyre and Argyll, and men from his own area of Carrick, Kyle and Cunningham. It was a truly national army with many Clans taking part, including Camerons, Campbells, Frasers, Gordons, Macphersons, MacLeans, MacGregors, Mackenzies, Ross' and Sinclairs.

The king set up his supply base at Cambuskenneth, in the loop of the Forth, not far from the castle.

On the 17th of June the English army left its southern bases and marched to Edinburgh. On the 22nd they left Edinburgh for Falkirk.

The next morning they set out for Stirling along the line of the old Roman road. They still had two days in which to relieve the castle, which could be clearly seen and which drew all eyes.

To start with Bruce kept his strongest division as a rearguard at the Torwood, between Stirling and Falkirk, with horse-patrols keeping an eye on the enemy. His main troops busied themselves preparing defensive positions covering Stirling.

They made skilful use of the line of the Bannockburn, and of the marshes and bogs which were then plentiful. He ordered pits to be dug, with spikes called calthrops placed inside, and for the pits to be covered so that they would maim the horses and the charging English knights.

His main position was a good one just inside the line of the New Park, between the Borestone and Bannockburn. His right wing was partly hidden in scrub and forest and his left along an escarpment which gave him good observation.

His plan would force King Edward to attack from the front over difficult ground for horses or to risk going round the left flank over other difficult terrain. If King Edward were to take the left flank, Bruce thought it might present a good opportunity to attack.

Later Bruce withdrew his division from the Torwood into his main position, to hold the edge of the wood in the New Park. He kept horse patrols out in front.

Edward Bruce's men held the high ground to the left, Moray was stationed near St Ninian's Church to watch the flat ground of the Carse. The rest were kept in the Borestone area (near the present Rotunda site). Tradition has it that the present Rotunda site where the Bruce statue is situated was Bruce's command post during part of the battle.

The ill-disciplined small-folk, panting to get at the enemy, were stationed behind Coxet Hill.

From the battlements of the castle, the anxious defenders peered, watching the sun glint on spears and armour, seeing clouds of dust and flags and pennants, and tried to unravel what the manoeuverings might mean, and whether they would be dead or alive in the next day or two.

They now knew with certainty that one of Scotland's greatest battles was about to take place.

Robert the Bruce - Kings of Scots

Victory at Bannockburn

The main body of the defenders of Stirling Castle joined their sentries on the battlements at first light on June 23, 1314 but they could discern little amid the trees and bogs.

Then they saw what appeared to be several hundred knights riding along the edge of the carse as if they were trying to get between the Scots army and the castle.

King Edward had ordered them to take up a position where they could harass the Scots once he had carried out his plan to dislodge them with a mammoth frontal assault.

Meanwhile, the van of the main body of cavalry, foot and archers led by the Earl of Hereford and the Earl of Gloucester, moved slowly towards the Scots. Bruce, unarmoured and mounted on a light pony, inspected his forward troops while still keeping a wary eye on the enemy. He accidentally strayed too far from his own lines.

One of the English knights, Sir Henry de Bohun, recognised the King by the coronet he was wearing on his helmet and suddenly left his own men and charged towards him. Bruce's commanders watched helplessly. They were too far away to go to his aid. Then alarm changed to exaltation. Bruce waited until the lance point was almost at his chest, then quickly wheeled the pony, dodged the lance, and split de Bohun's helmet and skull with his light battle-axe. A great cheer went up from the Scots troops.

On being reproved by his commanders for risking his life so near to the fighting, he merely remarked: "Alas, I have broken my good battle-axe".

The elated Scots troops charged the English advance guards and drove them back against the main body. Horses screamed and reared as they stepped on the pointed calthrops in the pits. Many others were deliberately lanced or hacked by the Scots to bring down their armoured riders.

The dust rose and fell and, when it cleared, the castle defenders saw the van of the English army falling back.

The Scots, under the tight control of the king, held their positions in the wood of the New Park and were greatly heartened by their initial success.

Meanwhile, the English force under Clifford and de Bowmont, sent along the edge of the carse, had not been seen by Moray's division, whose duty it was to guard that side. He was reprimanded by Bruce who sent messengers to warn him. "A rose has fallen from your chaplet," he said.

The stung Moray hurried his schiltrons down to the low ground. The Scots' careful training began to prove itself as they moved quickly in disciplined bodies, spears at the ready.

The English knights then charged the on-coming Scots who formed a dour and resolute hedgehog, and a desperate fight took place.

Knights flung maces and axes into the Scots ring, trying to force an opening so that they could use the weight of their horses, but the sweating spearsmen held firm. Douglas became anxious about his hard-pressed comrades, but the king told him to hold his own position and not to go to Moray's aid.

Then the Scots got their second wind, and as the English knights withdrew slightly they quickly broke the ring, formed their attack formation and moved forward with their long spears ready to strike.

The castle defenders, trying to make sense of the affray, suddenly saw the English force break up, one half galloping back to the main body, the other heading for the castle. The gates were quickly opened, and the English cavalry clattered in, many of the horses with spear wounds and some carrying wounded men slumped over the horses' heads or grimly clinging to the reins. They joined the defenders of the castle they had so eagerly hoped to relieve.

The Scots were pleased with themselves, and their success in these probing skirmishes. They had shown that their footsoldiers could beat off an attack by charging knights, and that their often-practised drills were effective in all-out war. They had killed Clifford, one of the commanders of the cavalry force. They had broken up and dislodged the force of knights King Edward had sent to place themselves strategically to the Scots rear, ready to strike when the moment was right. And they had blocked the advance of the van of the English army and had sent it reeling back. The opening phases of the battle had gone the Scots' way.

Bruce's success in single combat had also been a great morale booster.

King Edward called an urgent council of war. His angry commanders pointed out that they could only dislodge the Scots from the New Park trees and scrub with great difficulty because the position was such a strong one. They could not easily work round to the right in a flanking movement because of the nature of the terrain. The English soldiers were tired because of their long, forced marches to try and get to Stirling by the pledged date.

In the middle of all the heated talking and debate, the flaps of the headquarters tent parted and a man in a dark cloak entered. It was Sir Philip Mowbray, the commander of the castle. He had sneaked out, evaded the Scots sentries, and insisted to King Edward that the castle was now technically relieved.

But King Edward, angered by the day's reverses, wanted victory. He also needed larger supplies of drinking water for his huge numbers of men and horses, so he decided to move nearer to Stirling.

He planned to cross the Bannockburn and move towards the Forth, and relieve the castle the next day. King Edward was sure that Bruce, with his much smaller army, would not leave his prepared positions and attack him.

But Bruce was a superb tactician, and knew his ground. He knew that the carse ground was low-lying, rough, cut by the Bannockburn and the Pelstream, and by ditches and pools. At that time the banks of these burns were steep and the bottom soft and muddy. There were many bogs, and part of the Bannockburn was tidal where it joined the Forth.

King Edward moved into this rough territory to get to drier ground and his weary troops bivouacked for the night. It took a long time to transfer such large numbers of men to the drier ground, and reports say the wagons could not be moved and the troops had no food.

The English soldiers slept badly, and there were false alarms because the sentries were edgy about the possibility of a Scots night attack.

Bruce had considered breaking off the battle, taking his men into the hills of the west and continuing his guerilla warfare. But a Scots knight who had been in King Edward's army deserted and told Bruce that English morale was low and that their position in the carse was uncomfortable and disorganised.

Bruce now knew that because of the nature of the ground, the English army could not easily manoeuvre, and that the cavalry would be hampered. This would greatly reduce the English superiority in numbers.

He decided to attack them across the carse with Edward Bruce's division on the right, then Moray and Douglas, each slightly back to the left. His own division would be the reserve.

A force made up of civilians, and known as 'the small folk', was moved to the edge of the escarpment as a further reserve but possibly just to keep them out of the way. With such limited ground for movement an ill-disciplined mob could be a major hindrance. The few Scottish horsemen were kept well hidden.

June 24 was a sunny day, and the castle defenders, still keeping their anxious vigil, saw the Scots move down from their strong positions on to the flat ground.

It was St. John's Day, and the army attended Mass said by their chaplains. They knelt in prayer, almost within bow shot of the English army. Reports say that King Edward exclaimed: "They kneel for mercy!" But an English knight replied: "Yes, sire, but not from you—they mean to attack".

Quickly, King Edward ordered his knights to saddle and his bowmen drove off the few Scottish archers who were out in front of their advancing spearmen.

The Earl of Gloucester commanded the van of the main English body, and he ordered a charge. Edward Bruce's men skilfully and doggedly formed a hedgehog, and the charge perished in a welter of whinnying horses, broken spears, the screams and shouts of wounded and dying men. Gloucester was killed by the Scots spearmen, and the charge was halted.

Moray's division came storming up on the left and crashed into the English van. It broke and fell back on the main body.

The main armies now clanged together in a melee of hacking, swearing, shouting men, and the archers on both sides could not fire for fear of hitting their own comrades. Douglas's men, too, pushed forward in formation until the three Scottish divisions were all engaged in hectic hand-to-hand combat.

The Scots were inferior in numbers, but the narrowness of the front prevented the English army from widening out. The water obstacles, the broken ground, the steady pressure from the front, began to cause chaos. Orders were not passed. Men became confused. Those at the front were fiercely engaged. Those behind, pressed in mass, could not reach their enemy, nor manoeuvre.

The Scottish spearmen kept up the pressure. Their experience and training told, and as they were getting the necessary weight to press home their attack, the long spears caused havoc.

But the English army, which contained many brave and skilled soldiers, managed to get a body of archers out on the Scots left, and a hail of arrows began to open up gaps in the Scottish ranks.

For a moment it looked as if it was to be like the battle of Falkirk all over again, but Bruce sent an urgent message to Keith to charge with his few horsemen. The Scottish cavalry, small in number, had been anxiously watching the fighting, and given their chance, they charged the archers, scattered them and drove them from the field.

A dangerous moment had passed, and the Scots attack regained its momentum.

Bruce now turned to the MacDonalds and the men of the Western Isles in his own and strongest division. To their chief, Angus Og, he gave orders for them to attack and said: "My hope is constant in thee!"

This saying later became the motto of Clanranald, and the MacDonalds' behaviour at Bannockburn was to give them the automatic and proud place of right-of-the-line in Royal armies. (When they did not get it at Culloden, during the Jacobite Rising of 1745 they were so resentful that they did not fight with their normal resolution).

Bruce's timing was just right. His division charged into the press of men, and the English lines began to give ground under the renewed pressure.

The Scots scented victory, and the lines of spearmen began to press the main army back on those behind who could not help them because of the narrow front. The archers in the rear of the English army were out of effective range, and could not be called on in any meaningful way.

"On them, on them, they fail, they fail," shouted the Scots.

The Scottish spearmen kept up the pressure

Then came an incident which has now passed into legend. The small folk, the farmers, peasants, fishermen, the workmen, herders and huntsmen, with improvised weapons and no discipline, but who had been held in reserve on the escarpment, could stand the sight no more and poured over the edge. They pelted towards the fighting armies.

At the sight of what they took to be further Scottish reserves, the main mass of the English army gave way.

A disorganised retreat and near-massacre began.

King Edward was persuaded the day was lost, and retreated to Stirling Castle. One of his bravest knights, Sir Giles d'Argentine, who had been ordered to look after the king, saw him near to the castle and then said: "I am not accustomed to flee, nor am I going to begin now".

He returned to the battle, charged into the cheering on-coming Scots, and was killed.

The main mass of the English army broke towards the Forth. Many perished in the steep gorge of the Bannockburn. Others drowned in the pools and marshes and mud. In places men could walk on dead horses and corpses, forming a grisly bridge.

The English supply train was captured, valued at today's prices in the region of five to seven million pounds. English casualties were colossal. Nearly all archers and foot-soldiers being killed or captured, and many nobles and knights killed, or taken prisoner or held to ransom.

The slaughter went on for miles.

The Scots had suffered as well, particularly in the early fighting, but for them it was an overwhelming victory.

At the castle the demoralised garrison again opened the gates to let in a large contingent of fleeing English horsemen. Sir Philip Mowbray refused to permit King Edward to enter as he felt honour bound to surrender the castle.

The king escaped to Dunbar. A small boat took him to Berwick and England, and as the song says, "to think again". The next day the victorious Scots re-mustered at the castle, and the garrison surrendered.

Edward Bruce's rash promise had turned out successfully, and Stirling Castle—the main strategic fortress of Scotland—and the focal point of the battle was once again in the hands of the Scots in their quest for independence.

Murder and intrigue

One of the problems for a king long ago was that he had to struggle against powerful nobles. He often had to uneasily look over his shoulder, to play one faction against the other, to keep the balance of power, and yet to maintain his over-all position as sovereign.

It wasn't easy, and many a man ended his life in the dungeons or on the gallows or block because he strayed too far and incurred either the king's anger or the ire of one of the great families.

King James II had a red mark on his face, and was known as "Fiery Face". He also had a fiery temper, and the defiance of some of his nobles sometimes produced outbursts of a terrible anger.

He was determined to bring peace to his troubled realm and he re-enacted some of the laws from his father's reign, and added some others. He issued proclamations for keeping the peace, and penalties for rebellion and treason.

James wanted to show he was going to be firm, and he was uneasy about the growing power of the Douglases and other leading families. He had good reason for as a young boy he had been a pawn in the hands of the great nobles.

It could not be said that King James II had a pleasant start to life: his father had been murdered by the Grahams in Blackfriars Monastery in Perth when he was only six.

He could not be crowned at Scone, the usual place for Scottish Kings, because of fears for his safety. Instead the ceremony was performed in the chapel at Holyrood Palace.

His mother was virtually a prisoner of Sir William Crichton, governor of Edinburgh Castle, but the queen managed to outwit him and get herself and the young King to Stirling Castle.

She asked leave to go on pilgrimage to a particular church to pray for her son: she was permitted to take two boxes for her luggage. The queen put James in one box and her luggage in the other, and fled to Stirling.

Even there, he was in peril. Sir Alexander Livingstone was governor at Stirling and he, like Sir William Crichton, sought to be the leading man in the Kingdom.

The queen was told that both she and the boy-King must do as they were told, even although Archibald, Earl of Douglas, had been nominally appointed the King's lieutenant. (This particular member of the renowned and feared Douglas family turned out to be weak and indecisive).

The two ambitious castle governors then pretended to be friends and planned to divide power between them but their private pact broke up.

Sir William Crichton, at Edinburgh, schemed to get direct control of the King once again. He knew that James went hunting near Stirling Castle and he had him watched and his movements timed and noted. Then, one night, he hid himself and his men in the bushes and when morning came and the King went out with only a few attendants he found himself surrounded by armed men.

The young King was told that he was to return to Edinburgh Castle for his own protection.

The self-seeking planning of the nobles went on, and the two castle governors made yet another pact with one another. This time their new enemy was William, Earl of Douglas, who had succeeded the King's lieutenant to the huge Douglas estates.

The governors feared Douglas power, and it was therefore in their own interests to temporarily join up and oppose or kill him. Doubtless, each had plans to deal with the other once Douglas was out of the way.

The young King James was then forced to preside over an infamous deed of treachery, and perhaps it was that which made him act as he did at Stirling Castle many years later.

William, Earl of Douglas, was 18, vigorous and bold, when he, his brother David (his heir) and another relative were invited to Edinburgh Castle, probably in the King's name. When they got there they were hospitably received.

The Douglases were uneasy as there seemed to be a great many Crichton and Livingstone retainers around, but they were reassured by the behaviour of the young boy-King who appeared to be enjoying their company and who was unaware of the nobles' plot.

Then Sir William Crichton and Sir Alexander Livingstone accused Earl Douglas of being a traitor, and legend has it that a bull's head was placed on the table during the meal. This was a sign for the governors' men to seize the Douglases and to bind them.

Young King James protested and wept at the arrest of these friendly guests, but he was forced to preside at a mock trial after which the Douglases were quickly beheaded.

But the Douglases were not finished, and they were to ultimately prove a sore trial to James II.

The estates eventually came to another Earl William, who was to be one of the greatest and most notorious leaders of that belligerent family. William sided with Livingstone against Crichton, and the nation of Scotland was plagued by power struggles, plundering, internal war and lawlessness.

The situation worsened. Bishop James Kennedy of St. Andrews, a nephew of James I, feared that the Douglases would become so powerful that they would equal or replace the King. So he teamed up with Sir William Crichton. The strife spread as the powerful Earl of Crawford joined Douglas and laid waste the bishop's diocese. The bishop excommunicated the Earl, who did not seem unduly perturbed, but who later died in a skirmish. So the strife went on.

Young King James—lucky to survive—married Mary of Gueldres, in Holland, when he was 19 and set out to put his country to rights, and to curb the power of the great families.

Suddenly, he jailed all the leading members of the Livingstone family, took their lands and arranged a trial. The father was kept in prison and the sons were executed.

Then he turned his attention to the Douglases.

They had mammoth estates in central and southern Scotland. They could muster armies almost as large as the King's. Earl William had two brothers who were also earls. All were experienced in war against the English, and collectively they were among the most powerful factions in the land.

An old saying stated that no one dared touch a Douglas or a Douglas man.

But the King was astute. His spies told him that Earl William had made a secret alliance with the Earl of Ross and the new—and notoriously cruel—Earl of Crawford.

King James had already shown the Douglas that he was not to be trifled with for when the Earl was abroad the King had attacked and taken Douglas Craig, one of the earl's castles. He beseiged others, and forced Douglas' men to swear loyalty to the crown.

When the Earl returned, he felt it wise to bow for the moment to the King. James, perhaps thinking of the terrible bull's head dinner so many years ago, relented and returned Douglas' estates in the hope that this reconciliation would bring peace.

Then the King heard that Douglas had begun to intrigue with the

English, and he was greatly angered. The King was also infuriated by an incident when the nephew of Sir Patrick Gray, captain of the King's Guard, was imprisoned by Douglas because he had refused to join Douglas in his wild affrays and his defiance of the King's laws.

The King sent Sir Patrick to Threave Castle to ask for his release. The Earl received Sir Patrick civilly, and quoted an old proverb about its being ill talking between a full man and fasting, and refused to discuss any business until Sir Patrick had eaten.

Douglas then read the King's letter. Douglas said that the prisoner, MacLellan, the tutor of the young laird of Bombie, would be put at Sir Patrick's disposal. He then presented him with MacLellan—minus his head which had been removed during lunch.

Sir Patrick calmly withdrew, but once outside the gates he flung his gauntlet at the castle walls, cursed Douglas, and rode for his life.

Douglas also infuriated James by; 1, Holding his own parliament and forbidding people to attend the official one; 2, A flow of high-handed actions, including the murder and hanging of the King's friends.

The King, his patience sorely tried, invited Douglas to Stirling Castle and promised him safe conduct in a letter under the privy seal.

Douglas came with only a handful of attendants on February 21, 1452. He was received well and entertained to dinner and supper on the following day.

After supper, about seven o' clock in the evening, the king led him to an inner chamber. He decided to have it out, as we would say nowadays, and he challenged Douglas about the bond between himself and the Earls of Crawford and Ross.

Douglas refused all questions. The discussion grew heated. They were both young men: the King was 21, Douglas 26, and they had the impatience of youth as well as living in a violent age. The King demanded answers. Douglas still refused.

Perhaps he felt secure in the knowledge of safe conduct, and once he was back on his own lands he could muster almost as many men as the king.

Tempers flared, and the king - his fiery temper now at boiling point and with all thought of safe conduct gone - drew a knife. He shouted: "False traitor, if you will not break the bond I shall", and plunged his knife twice into Earl William's body.

Hearing the uproar, Sir Patrick Gray, Sir Alexander Boyd, Stewart

In a rage - the King drew a knife

of Darnley and other courtiers rushed in. Sir Patrick, the same man whose nephew had been murdered by Douglas and who had flung his gauntlet at the walls of Threave Castle, struck him with a pike. The others also stabbed Earl William, and his body was hurled out of a window.

There was consternation in the land when the news spread. Many thought the king had blundered, to slay without a trial. He had broken his word, rumour said. People were scandalised: the king was well liked by the common people. He would go among them, was accessible to them, and at times shared the rations and the quarters of the ordinary soldiers.

James Douglas, brother of the murdered man and the new Earl, rode to Stirling with 600 men. They sacked and burned houses, roughed up the terrified townspeople, exhibited in public the letter of safe conduct and dragged it through Stirling attached to a horse's tail. It was open defiance of the King of Scots.

James Douglas also put the King "to the horn", a grave insult. In Scotland at that time when a person refused to obey the law a horn was blown three times at the town cross and that meant the person was now an outlaw. The Douglases were in fact saying that they considered the King to be King no longer.

The king's throne, reputation and effectiveness were in grave danger. It is said that the King was so overcome with horror that he spoke of giving up the struggle against the nobles and of flying as a refugee to France.

But his friends reminded him of the old tale of the sheaf of arrows - unbreakable when they were tied together, easily broken one by one. So the King resolved to deal with the other nobles on that basis.

He set out to re-establish himself. He had marched north with an army against the Earl ofCrawford, and found he had already been defeated by the Earl of Huntly.

On June 12, 1452, in Parliament at Edinburgh the King was cleared of giving Douglas safe conduct. Parliament felt Douglas' traitorous refusal to name the bond meant he was guilty of his own death "by refusing the King's gentle persuasion."

The King was absolved of breach of faith, and the Douglas was declared to have been justly put to death.

Meanwhile, the Douglases were still, literally, up in arms. They posted letters of defiance on the doors of Parliament Hall.

But royal retribution was again to fall on them.

The King conferred favours and titles on the nobles and Church men who had supported him, and ensured their support. He headed south with an army of 30,000 men and laid waste to the Douglas lands of Peebles, Selkirk and Dumfries. Ultimately, James, the new Earl of Douglas, submitted to the King.

The King then turned his attention to the north. The Earl of Crawford submitted and terms were made with Ross as well. The formidable alliance of the three earls ended.

All now seemed calm with the King again in the ascendency. But the Douglases still simmered, and King James's spies again told him that the new Earl of Douglas was scheming and intriguing against the throne. James resolved to crush them once and for all.

In March, 1455, he marched south again, burned crops and buildings, captured and sacked castles. Douglases' three brothers were defeated. The key leaders had their heads cut off.

When Parliament again met on June 9, 1455, Douglas, his mother, the Countess Beatrice, and three brothers were all attainted and their estates forfeited.

Parliament then passed sweeping acts effectively giving the king the right to all key castles. He took the lands of Douglas, Crawford and Ross, and was virtually an unchallenged monarch.

The weak boy-King had become strong, warlike and clever, and he survived in an age of turbulence and intrigue. His death, not surprisingly, was in war. He was killed in 1460 when a cannon exploded at the seige of Roxburgh during the wars against the English. He was 29.

You can still see the room in Stirling Castle today where James II stabbed the Douglas.

The buildings overlooking the lawn do not contain the chamber where the Earl supped with the King: fire destroyed many apartments in later years. But a small room where the stabbing took place survived.

It is sited above an old archway, and the window still exists through which the bloodcovered body was hurled after 'Fiery Face' lost his temper.

The secrets of King James V

From the battlements of Stirling Castle you can see blue hills, green fields and woods, the silver links of the River Forth and many towns, villages and farms.

If you wonder what kind of people live there, how they earn their living and what they are really like, you will be following the thought processes of a Scottish monarch many centuries ago.

It is said that James V became so wearied of the life of the court, of the flatteries of men and women out for self-advancement, of the restrictions of protocol and formal behaviour that he rebelled.

He wanted to really know what his people were like. So he decided to find out. He slipped out of the castle in disguise and explored the town and countryside.

He was a daring person, and had been brought up in a hard school.

James V was born in Linlithgow in 1513 and was brought at an early age to Stirling. He spent much of his early life in Edinburgh Castle but Stirling was his favourite.

His father had fallen with the flower of Scottish chivalry at the disastrous battle of Flodden, and James V came to the throne as a two-year-old boy in troubled times. Scotland was beset by power-struggles among the great families and with intermittent war against England.

One of the branches of the famed Douglas family, the Red Douglases, virtually ruled the country for a time and kept the young King a prisoner. They treated him so harshly that he never forgot it, and he determined to break their power.

He planned a daring escape. When at Falkland Palace he told the Douglases he would be going hunting the next morning and that he wanted to go to bed early.

In the middle of the night, he slipped on his clothes, crept out to the stable, and silently obtained three horses for himself and two personal servants. Then they galloped for their lives to the safety of Stirling Castle.

It was not surprising a King that could so look after himself could devise a plan to wander the countryside and get to know the people.

As a grown man, he talked with farmers, herdsmen, hunters and the packmen and their wives. They did not know who he was. He pretended to be a minor laird and enjoyed himself sharing the customs and the hospitali-

The King often won prizes in wrestling matches

ty of his subjects.

He got on well with people. The records of the time say he was not tall, but he was strong. He had a sharp wit, courteous manners, ate sparely and seldom drank wine. He had red hair, and the people called him the "Red Tod" or the "Red Fox".

It was said he could withstand cold, heat and hunger with a good humour, and that one of his main faults was a tendency towards romance and amours, a fairly common vice of the time.

It was also said that he was considerate, and ensured that any children of his liaisons were well cared for and their mothers given financial aid.

The King was also fond of music and poetry and records show accounts-entries for lutes, and lute strings, for viols and repairs to an organ.

He had been greatly influenced as a youth by Sir David Lyndsay of the Mount, Lord Lyon King-at-Arms, a poet of great repute in his day.

He was an enthusiastic patron of the popular Mayday pastimes and games, attended plays and festivals and won and gave prizes for archery and wrestling. He enjoyed field sports, and had a passion for horses.

It was little wonder the people respected him and gave him the affectionate title of "King of the Commons".

James V planned his incognito journeyings with great care. He gave himself the title of "Gudeman of Ballengeich" from the steep path leading to the main town, on the north-west side of the castle, where the present Ballengeich road is now situated. It separates the castle from the Gowan Hill.

The ancient gateway to the castle, erected by Robert II and now built-up, was sited there. The name means the stormy or windy pass, and was probably originally written as Ballochgiech. Gudeman was a description applied to a class of small proprietors who held their land, not from the crown, but from a vassal.

It was a wise choice by the King. Enough rank to explain his bearing and manners. Not too high to discourage friendly and intimate relationships with the common people.

The incidents of his wanderings became the subject of many a legend, and were told in ballad and song, such as "The Gaberlunzie Man" and "We'll Gang Nae Mair A-Roving".

He did not always travel for the purposes of gallantry or the love of personal adventure. There are stories of him dealing out summary justice to known wrongdoers, and of attacking bandits either single-handed or with a few attendants.

Sir Walter Scott drew on fact in his epic poem "The Lady of the Lake" when he described the famous single combat fight between the King as Fitzjames and the Highland chieftain, Rhoderick Dhu.

Once when the King was out hunting he was separated from his attendants and entered a cottage in the middle of a moor not far from the foot of the Ochil Hills. He was not recognised and was kindly received.

The farmer told his wife to fetch the hen that roosted nearest the cock, which is always the plumpest, for the stranger's supper.

The King was highly pleased with his food and the company and told his host that he would return his kindness. He told the farmer that when he next came to Stirling he should call at the castle and ask for the Gudeman of Ballengeich.

He did so, and was astounded to discover that he had entertained the King. In front of laughing courtiers, the King entertained him... and then lightheartedly gave him the title King of the Moors.

Legend has it that the King visited a miller's house near Falkland, and got on so well that he jokingly asked the miller whether he would like the fourth part, the eighth or the sixteenth part of the lands on which they stood.

The miller is said to have lightheartedly replied that the sixteenth was over greedy, the fourth part would be cheating himself and he would strike between the two and ask for nothing.

Laughing, the King identified himself... and gave him the eighth part. Although he could be tough with serious wrongdoers, he could take a joke, as the modern saying has it.

The King of Kippen

Carriers taking royal goods to Stirling took a route which passed the house of Buchanan of Arnprior. The laird, who could be a law unto himself, asked one of the carriers to dump his load and he would pay him for it.

The carrier refused, telling him that his goods were for the King. Buchanan then took the goods by force. "

If King James is King of Scotland then I am King of Kippen," he said. It was reasonable, he said, that the King should share his goods with his neighbour-king.

The alarmed and empty-handed carrier fled to the castle and complained to the king's servants, who informed James.

Off set the angry King for Kippen, accompanied by a few retainers. He demanded access to Buchanan's house, but was refused by a man carrying a battleaxe who said there could be no access until dinner was over.

The King asked again, and got another blunt refusal. Then he told the man to tell his master that the Gudeman of Ballengeich desired to speak with the King of Kippen.

Out came Buchanan of Arnprior and was astounded to recognise his sovereign. Both men laughed. The King entered, and Buchanan entertained him so well that they became firm friends and the King gave him leave to take what he wanted when the royal carts were passing his door.

Buchanan was asked to the castle, and to the enjoyment of all was treated as the King of Kippen.

There is another story that when the King was residing at Holyrood Palace he was attacked by four or five footpads when returning from one of his private jaunts.

He took a stance on a high and narrow bridge over the River Almond and defended himself with a light sword.

A peasant, threshing in a nearby farm, heard the noise and joined what he thought was the weaker man. He laid about with a flail, and the robbers fled.

He invited James into his barn where the King asked for a basin and towel. The King found out through casual conversation that his new friend's dearest earthly wish was to possess his farm upon which he worked as a bondsman. The lands belonged to the Crown.

James did not tell him who he was, but invited the man to come to

Holyrood and ask for the Gudeman of Ballengeich.

The man eventually came and the King revealed himself. He presented his helper with the farm lands under the service of presenting an ewer, basin and towel for the King to wash his hands when he should happen to pass the Bridge of Cramond.

The stories of the wandering king, romantic, hardy, good-humoured and at ease with all people, lasted for centuries.

He had not had an easy life, and he did not succeed in achieving his national wishes for himself or his people. There were too many major difficulties facing him, resolute though he was.

As an adult, he had plenty of trouble on his hands. He said Scotland was not big enough to hold him and the Douglases and he initially restricted their area of influence. They were not to come within six miles of him. Then he had their estates seized, and banished them from the country.

He did his best to bring law and order to the unruly Border country, including the summary hanging of the head of the powerful Armstrong family.

He dealt with the Clan chiefs in the Highlands in the same way — making friends with some, punishing others.

He had constant friction with Henry VIII over his war with France and the mammoth events of the Reformation.

James was determined for political and religious reasons to stay friendly with France, and in 1536 he married Madelaine, daughter of King Francis I, with that aim in mind. Sadly, she died not long afterwards.

Henry VIII was infuriated once more when two years later James married another French woman, Mary of Lorraine, who became the mother of Mary, Queen of Scots.

War broke out between Scotland and England, and because of disorganisation, quarrels over leadership and lack of planning the Scots were easily routed by a smaller English army at the battle of Solway Moss.

These events broke James's health and nerve. His only two lawful children died, and he took himself to Falkland Palace where he died in 1542 shortly after hearing that a daughter had been born to him, the future and ill-fated Mary Queen of Scots.

He is said to have uttered the oft-quoted words: "It cam' wi' a lass, and it will gang wi' a lass", meaning that the crown that had come to the Stewarts by a woman, Marjorie Bruce, daughter of King Robert I, would be lost through the girl that had just been born.

Poor James! He felt his life had been a failure.

Yet there are lasting memorials to him. He set up the Court of Session in Edinburgh, Scotland's greatest civil law court, which operates to this day. And in Stirling Castle there are stories in stone, the great palace that he built and a statue at the corner of the wall next to the Great by Hall.

The Palace windows are surmounted by stones showing I 5 for James V.

The figure at the corner is thought to show the King disguised as the Gudeman o' Ballengeich.

The "King of the Commons" is not forgotten either in legend or amid the mementoes of history.

The mighty ship of Stirling Castle

There was tremendous excitement in the castle and the town. Torches flared. Trumpets blew. Messengers clattered off on horseback. The townspeople poured out of the houses to see what the fuss was about.

They told one another of the great news. A son had been born to the King.

It meant a great deal because James VI was now 28 and the continuance of the Scottish crown in the house of Stewart had seemed a precarious thing.

The King and his Queen, Anne of Denmark, rejoiced that February day in 1593-4.

The baby was to become Henry, Prince and Steward of Scotland and Duke of Rothesay. He was also created Prince of Wales in 1610, but sadly he did not live to succeed to the crowns of Scotland and England. He died aged 18, not long after James had become King of England as well as Scotland. Still, at the time of the birth, hopes ran high for a glorious future.

It was no surprise when the king and queen decided to make the baptism of Prince Henry a great occasion.

Their celebration became the talk of European courts.

Preparations began months ahead. Royalty from other lands and ambassadors were invited to attend. Large sums were spent on their accommodation and entertainment. The King built the Chapel Royal in Stirling Castle specifically for the baptism, replacing an earlier chapel in bad repair. Scotland wanted to do the occasion justice.

As with a major royal event today, no expense was spared. Every co-operation from townspeople was expected to ensure that all went well on the day.

All the leading Scottish nobles were asked to attend and any who did not were in disfavour for a long time to come.

The King wanted a peaceful and joyful celebration, but there were problems. Rivalries between great families, clans and houses could easily lead to quarrels and blows with so many retainers and soldiers flocking around castle and town, each eager to demonstrate his own master's importance and recalling old feuds.

The King issued a special proclamation. It was read at the Mercat Cross of Stirling on August 24. Three heralds and two trumpeters took part

The proclamation was read at the Mercat Cross

to emphasise its importance.

The message was unmistakable. No matter the rank, high or low, the king expected no brawling. He demanded good behaviour, courtesy to the visiting ambassadors and their retainers, and urged that the nobles should select servants who were well-behaved. All this should be done for the good name of Scotland.

The baptism was delayed for some days because the Queen of England's special envoy was ill and his replacement was held up by bad weather.

When it did take place there was much to marvel at. There were tournaments which delighted the crowds, and a splendid banquet. Rooms were hung with velvet and taffeta or cloth-of-gold. Rich presents were given, and honours bestowed.

But it was the events which were to take place inside the Great Hall of Stirling Castle which were to set the tongues wagging.

A huge gathering sat down to the banquet, with the King, the Queen and ambassadors at a top table. All could see down the middle of the hall.

Great care had been taken with seating arrangements. A lady of high rank was seated between each noble and overseas visitor.

After the first course the trumpets played a fanfare, and there was then appreciative murmuring from the guests. The second course, a dessert, was carried in on a table placed on a chariot twelve feet long and seven broad.

The chariot was moved by men hidden within it and screened from the guests by hanging cloths. It was led by a blackamoor dressed in rich clothes and wearing a harness of pure gold.

It was accompanied by six ladies, three in white satin and three in crimson, with feathers and jewels on their heads. Each lady carried a badge to denote her identity, plus a motto. They represented Ceres, the goddess of agriculture and civilisation, and such themes as Fecundity, Faith, Concord, Liberality and Perseverance.

They served dessert to the guests, and then they and the chariot left the hall, amid applause.

The King had originally intended to have the chariot drawn by a real lion which had been brought specially from Holyroodhouse, but the idea was dropped, possibly because of the danger to the guests.

But more was to follow.

The third course was of fish, crabs, lobster and shellfish made with sugar and brought in a way that led to cheers, clapping and gasps of amusement.

An immense "ship" appeared from behind screens to another fanfare of trumpets. It was 18 feet long, eight wide, and forty feet to the top of the masts and flags. It was mounted on a wheeled base designed to depict the sea, and weighed several tons. A lady stood at her helm, wearing cloth of gold, and appeared to guide the ship.

Many men were hidden inside heaving at levers and wheels. Over 30 people crowded her decks, waving to the guests and performing seamanlike tasks.

The pilot and five seamen wore special Spanish taffeta, fourteen musicians wore the royal colours of red and gold, and mythical and nautical characters—well-known to the people of that time, were depicted.

Arion with his harp who, myth said, had been rescued from the sea by dolphins. Neptune, God of the Sea, was there with his trident. So was Thetis, mother of Achilles, with her mace and Triton and the son of Neptune, with his trumpet. Neptune wore an Indian cloth of silver and silk, and the rest were also richly dressed.

The ship was also accompanied by other characters of the sea, ladies and girls dressed as sirens and mermaids. They wore pearls, coral, shells and precious metals.

In addition to this colourful and laughing crew, which received rapturous applause from the guests, the ship also had 36 brass guns.

There were political lessons for the guests.

The ship commemorated the King's voyage across the North Sea to fetch his bride from Scandinavia. Latin mottoes painted on the sails of white taffeta, or carried by the crew, helped emphasise the point

The royal colours added further weight. The masts were painted red. The rigging was of red silk, the blocks of gold and the anchors silver-gilt. The mainsail bore the arms of Scotland and Denmark and another sail bore the emblem of the North Star.

The trumpets blared again. There was more applause as the ship hoisted its sails and creaked its way up the hall to the top table. Then shouts of surprise and some alarm. A salute was fired from some of the guns which made many of the guests jump.

The musicians played with renewed vigour and the mermaids sang, and the audience quietened down again.

The ship 'sailed' to the high table, halted and dropped its anchor.

An immense ship appeared

More music followed. Arion, dressed like a dolphin, played his harp. There was more singing. The audience watched enraptured as Neptune supervised the unloading of the sugar-objects cargo.

There was more appreciative murmuring when it was seen that the food being carried was in beautifully fashioned and ornamented glasses.

The musicians continued to sing and play, and the whole crew sang a hymn of congratulations to the king, queen and prince. More music followed, including an appropriate psalm.

The departure of the ship was equally impressive. The anchor was raised, trumpets sounded, and the ship moved in stately fashion down the hall, while within her hidden and sweating workmen toiled at their wheels and levers. Just before she vanished behind the screens she fired all her remaining guns.

The fun was not yet over because the royal party and the guests adjourned to another hall to continue feasting until the early hours of the morning.

Special displays of this kind were not unknown at the time, but the Stirling ship was in a class of its own.

Reports tell of marvelling guests, and tales went back to many places in Europe of the Scottish skills in design and craftsmanship that had brought it about.

The English ambassadors did not mention it in their reports, possibly—some historians think—because they did not wish to arouse Queen Elizabeth's envy.

The ship was later stripped of its rich hangings and furnishings and it went into store. It was never used again, but later reports tell of it being in Stirling Castle nearly two centuries later.

Its memory stayed for a long time. Envoys and nobles, and the townspeople who heard of it from servants and workmen who had for many weeks and months built it and furnished it, felt deep pride that the Scottish court could put on such a show.

After that, the ship vanished, and no trace now remains of one of the castle's great events.

Last shots in anger

It used to be said that some of the older houses near Stirling Castle had nicks and gashes in the stonework, a relic of the days when shots were last fired in anger from the battlements.

It was not all that long ago. It happened when Prince Charles Edward Stuart's Jacobite army was retreating northwards towards the end of the 1745-46 Rising.

They had been in the vicinity before. When they marched south the previous September after the Prince had raised his Standard at Glenfinnan, in the West Highlands, they had passed within cannon shot of the castle.

The Clansmen had then marched in good order, with colours flying and pipes playing. The Hanoverian garrison had fired several shots, most of which fell short or passed harmlessly over. The Highlanders had jeered, and continued their triumphant march to Edinburgh, and their victory at Prestonpans.

But now in the bleak weather of January all was different. A new grimness was in the air. The Prince's army, en route to London, had decided to turn at Derby, a move hotly argued about to this day. London was in turmoil and it was possible that had the Highlanders kept going that they would have won all and re-established the Stuarts on the throne of Britain.

But the decision was taken to return to Scotland, to see the winter out, to try and capture the Hanoverian forts in the Highlands and then, when spring came, to burst out anew with a larger army drawn from the Clans sympathetic to the Stuart cause.

Many Stirling townspeople were opposed to the Prince, and a 400 strong militia was formed and given muskets and swords by the castle garrison.

General Blakeney, who commanded the castle, energetically put his defences in order. He blew up the southern arch of Stirling Bridge to prevent the Jacobites crossing.

The Prince hoped to capture the castle and established his headquarters at Bannockburn. He sent his best general, Lord George Murray, to Alloa to meet with Lord John Drummond who several days before had landed in the north-east with heavy artillery and stores from France, necessary if the Jacobites were to capture the Highland forts.

On January 4, 1746, the Prince's army occupied the outskirts of

Stirling and the next day he sent a letter to the town council, with a drummer boy, ordering the town to surrender. The militia, unused to the niceties of war protocol, fired on the boy and he ran away, leaving his drum.

A second letter was sent warning the town of dire consequences, and it surrendered on January 8.

The castle garrison continued to defy the prince.

There was much acrimony and recrimination later about the surrender. Those who wanted to fight said they had the support of the castle soldiers. Those who had counselled surrender argued that they had no strong defences, only slight dykes or hedges on some sides of the town, and the Prince had a battery of smaller cannon and larger cannon across the Forth. The town had no cannon at all.

The question of whether the Prince got his larger cannon or not from Alloa across the Forth was crucial to the fate of the castle.

The Hanoverian troops did what they could. They had broken the bridge, and they stationed sloops offshore at Alloa to prevent a crossing of the Forth there. General Henry Hawley, who was pursuing the Jacobites north, sent small boats and 300 men from Leith, including one with a small cannon, to attack the Jacobites on the shores of the Forth and to try to dislodge them.

It was a difficult job for the Prince's army to move their cannon, because they included heavy pieces: two 16-pounders, two 12-pounders and two 8-pounders.

There was skirmishing along the banks of the Forth, including a vigorous clash at Airth, and the Jacobites eventually sent their light cannon up to the Fords of Frew, an ancient crossing in the carseland about six miles from Stirling. Lord George Murray speedily brought men from Falkirk, where his main army was based, and set up four guns to command the south shore of the Forth.

The heavier cannons were loaded on a captured ship at Alloa.

The Jacobites bombarded the Hanoverian sloops from the shore and cut their cables, and they drifted down river on the tide. The way was clear, but there were still difficulties. One cannon alone weighed 1.75 tons and needed 20 horses to pull it.

Eventually all were brought near to the castle where General Blakeney's men kept watch and got ready to withstand the now-certain bombardment.

But trouble was to befall the Jacobite army. The Prince was advised

The Highlanders jeered as castle garrison fired shots

on artillery matters by two men, one a Scot, James Alexander Grant, and the other a Frenchman, Mirabelle de Gordon.

The Frenchman was an engineer, a Chevalier of the Order of St. Louis, and he had been sent to Scotland with Lord John Drummond. He was treated as a gunnery expert but his experience was limited.

Mr Grant wanted trenches dug and the guns established on ground at the side of the town, opposite the castle gate and beside the present cemetery and Holy Rude Church. It was a good position, reasonably well sheltered and within easy range.

The alarmed inhabitants protested that the site was too near dwelling houses. Monsignor Mirabelle's view then prevailed. He had trenches dug on the Gowan Hill, to the north of the castle, where there was only 15 inches of earth above solid rock. The exposed Jacobite gunners had to build barricades and shelters from bags of wool and sacks filled with earth.

They were quickly blasted out of their badly-chosen and ill-protected gun positions, and were forced to build higher and stronger barricades. Reports speak of them losing 25 men a day.

When the Prince called on the castle to surrender General Blakeney refused, with good reason. The garrison were standing firm and were as yet in no real peril.

By January 15 little progress had been made. By this time the Prince had a major battle on his hands because General Hawley was nearing Falkirk with a Hanoverian army, and it was clear the Highlanders would have to fight this determined and tough opponent.

The Prince was not short of men at this stage. He had at least 1,200 disposed at the castle and in Stirling, and almost 10,000 at Falkirk.

Thanks to brilliant generalship by Lord George Murray, the Highlanders fought—other than one indisciplined charge—a brave and controlled engagement and swept Hawley's army from the field, capturing much equipment and many prisoners, including the hangman which General Hawley had brought with him to execute Jacobites should they be defeated.

The Prince and his leaders discussed whether they should pursue General Hawley's fleeing army or continue the siege of Stirling Castle.

Mirabelle de Gordon advised them that the castle would surrender in a day or so, and the harassed Jacobite gunners had more trenches dug on the Gowan Hill and more barricades built. They managed to get three of their seven battering cannon in place.

On January 29 the cannons belched smoke and the crashing echoes reverberated around the town. The balls crashed into the castle walls, sending up showers of masonry and stones and causing serious damage. It began to look as if a breach would be made.

But General Blakeney quickly replied with his 9-pounders and dismounted the Jacobite guns and demolished most of their emplacements. Several of the Jacobite officers were deeply angered, for they had advised that Mirabelle should not open fire until all seven guns were ready.

There were many dead, and fierce quarrels broke out with Mirabelle.

As time passed men began to slip away from the Jacobite army, to take booty home, or to see to wife and family, and their cattle and small fields, but it was not desertion in the modern sense. It was understood they would return when they could, and certainly in the spring.

The chiefs advised Prince Charles to retreat into the Highlands. His army, they said, was not strong enough to stand another lowland engagement at the moment. They should try and take the Highland forts and re-muster in the spring.

Eventually, and sadly, the order was given for a retreat into the northern hills and glens.

It was an untidy retreat, so unlike the confident march south when the flags flew and the pipes played and the men cheered and jeered at the castle troops. The Clansmen straggled north by bands. The baggage carts and cannon were spiked and abandoned.

An ammunition dump at St Ninian's Church accidentally blew up and two local people were killed. Only the steeple was left. It can still be seen to this day.

The main force marched to Dunblane by the Fords of Frew, and then to the north.

From the battlements of Stirling Castle the soldiers of General Blakeney watched them go, and fired a few rounds in derision... the last shots in anger ever to be fired from Stirling Castle.

They saw the red and green tartans of the Stewarts and MacDonalds, the Camerons and the MacGregors, the McLarens, Farquharsons, Robertsons, the McGillivrays, the Macintoshes, and the other Clans who followed the Prince disappear into the distance.

They were also disappearing into history because it was to be the last time that a Stirling Castle garrison would see such an army on the

An ammunition dump at St. Ninian's church blew up

march.

On the day the Jacobites left, the advance guard of General (Butcher) Cumberland entered the town. The castle guns fired once more, but this time in salute.

The old bridge of Stirling was repaired, and the Hanoverian army left for the north and ultimately for the battlefield of Culloden, where the hopes of the House of Stuart were to be dashed for ever.

The shots fired at Stirling signalled the beginning of the end of the Gaelic and Highland way of life. They marked a new turn in the train of events that eventually led to the suppression of the tartan, of the power of the chiefs, to the complex factors which brought sweeping changes in Highland life and ultimately led to the Clearances, the emptying of the glens and mass emigration.

Stirling was often the focal point of so much that was significant in Scottish wars.

The gun-duel between General Blakeney's soldiers and the Jacobite artillerymen on the Gowan Hill was, in its own way, one of the turning points of the final Jacobite rising.

So, if you see scores and marks on old buildings or are lucky enough to find a musket or cannon ball buried in ground roundabout it will be a final memento of the last time guns were fired from the battlements of Stirling Castle, and the last time a beseiging army set out to capture this ancient fortress.

Dead men's view

Stirling Castle has many memories. Some are humorous, some gruesome and some are odd and puzzling.

As you walk round the battlements have a good look down to the ground below and you will wonder how John Damien only suffered a broken leg after he dived off the edge in a vain bid to fly. The exact spot is unknown but it is thought to be somewhere near the garden parapet.

It all happened in 1507, in the reign of King James IV.

John Damien, a Frenchman, was what today we would call an amateur scientist and what people then called an apothecary. He wormed his way into the King's favour, and among other experiments he attempted to turn base metals into gold.

The King was initially impressed and appointed him Abbot of Tungland, in Galloway, as a reward for his labours. Others were not so receptive and referred to him sarcastically as the "French leech", a reference both to his alleged medical skills and his attachment to the King.

After a time, King James grew disenchanted with him and Damien, alarmed at his waning popularity, endeavoured to get back into favour. He announced that he had made a pair of wings, and that he intended to fly off the castle walls and that he would be in France before the King's ambassadors could get there.

This plan was greeted with great excitement and some scepticism. A large crowd of nobles, retainers, soldiers and servants gathered at the battlements and, as the word spread, a mob of townspeople gathered at the bottom, warily looking upwards.

John Damien strapped on his large wings, made of light wood to which were attached many feathers from eagles wings, plus some from the wings of hens.

He stepped on to the edge of the battlements, and a hush fell. Then he sprang into the air and jumped off. There were cries of consternation as he plummeted downwards, arms flailing, and thudded into the ground.

The people below began to jeer as Damien was carried away.

He had been fortunate in escaping with only a fractured leg. Some reports say he broke his thigh bone. Damien blamed the accident on the fact that he had used some hens' feathers in the wings. They had coveted the midden, and not the skies, he said.

Damien plummeted towards the ground

The Scottish poet William Dunbar wrote a satirical poem about the event called "The Ballad of the Fenzeit Freir of Tungland".

Damien was said to be more deeply hurt by the mob's jeers and the ridicule of the court than the pain of his leg, but the story had a happy ending for him—the King was so taken by the amusement of the bizarre experiment and, possibly, by Damien's courage that he received him at court once more.

Odd happenings? Well, in the reign of Robert III a wearied stranger called Thomas Warde of Trumpington turned up at the castle.

He bore the marks of imprisonment and privation, and looked exactly like King Richard II of England. He had appeared at the court of the Lord of the Isles, at Islay, and was produced at Stirling as a person likely to be of advantage in time of strife with England.

King Richard's end was obscure and many people in Scotland and England thought he had escaped from prison.

Quite what the Scots hoped to get from the stranger is not clear, but for a long time a so-called King of England, known in history as the "Mammet" or the false King, lived in Stirling Castle. He died there in 1419.

He was not the only 'pretender' to visit Stirling. King James IV received in 1495 the imposter, Perkin Warbeck, and he was treated with great courtesy as the reputed son of Edward IV of England.

The Scottish nobles followed their monarch's example, and the Earl of Huntly even agreed to a marriage with his daughter.

Perkin Warbeck was given a large pension, and James made war on England on his behalf in 1496 and again the next year. But the deception could not last forever and relationships between Perkin Warbeck and the King became strained.

Perkin Warbeck eventually left Scotland for the south in 1497.

Gruesome tales? There are any number.

Take a walk to the Gowan Hills, where the two cannon from Napoleonic times sit beside the spot where people were beheaded in past centuries.

Look all round at the lovely hills, fields and woods. It must have been heart-breaking for many a man to kneel, or stand, hands bound, and look at that view and know that within a few minutes the swish and thud of the executioner's axe would shut his eyes for ever.

There are arguments over the meaning of the name Gowan Hills, but one theory is that it is from a Scots word for lamentation.

It was here King James I had some of Scotland's leading nobles executed. He was a man of firm resolve, and determined to curb lawlessness in the country, whether it was by warring nobles or by common robbers and thieves.

In 1424 he had returned to his native land 18 years after being captured as a boy by the English when on his way to France. On his return, he uttered the famous words: "If God grants me life, I will make the key keep the castle and the bracken-bush the cow". In other words, the laws of the realm were to be obeyed by all.

A year after his coronation at Scone King James held court at Stirling Castle in May, 1425, and drastic measures followed.

He had little love for his cousin, the Regent Murdoch, Duke of Albany, or his family, for they had kept his father and grandfather from ruling, and had control of Scotland when he was prisoner in England.

The King also probably believed that the Albany family were responsible for starving his brother, David, to death, and that they may have prolonged his imprisonment by the English in the hope of taking the throne. The King also feared their power and perhaps he had cast covetous eyes at their large estates. Whatever the reason, or combination of reasons, the outcome was swift and straightforward.

He jailed Duke Murdoch's eldest son, Walter Stewart, on a charge of robbery, and followed that up by imprisoning Duncan, Earl of Lennox, the father of Duke Murdoch's wife.

For good measure, he then imprisoned Duke Murdoch himself, his wife and another son. Not surprisingly, there were repercussions and another of the Duke's sons gathered a small army, attacked the town of Dumbarton, killed townspeople, burned houses and slew the Keeper of Dumbarton Castle.

Duke Murdoch, his two sons, and the Earl of Lennox were summarily tried by the King. They were brought to the Heading Hill on the Gowan Hills and beheaded.

Tales abounded in Scotland of the King's severity and determination. After dealing with the Albany family he turned his attention to the powerful and unruly clan chiefs of the Highlands and Islands.

He summoned them to a parliament at Inverness, and when they attended—including Alexander, Lord of the Isles—James immediately ordered the arrest of the 40 leading chiefs. He jailed most of them, and had the most dangerous executed.

Inevitably, he made implacable enemies.

The Gowan Hills at Stirling were to figure in a horrible way in an event not long after the King's death.

He had incurred the hatred of Sir Robert Graham, whom he had jailed for a time, and he had also taken Graham lands. The Grahams and other nobles who hated the King plotted to kill him.

Then followed the well-known story of James' assassination in the Blackfriars Monastery at Perth where he went to spend Christmas in 1436. The King's chamberlain, Sir Robert Stewart, the Master of Atholl, betrayed him, laid planks across the monastery moat and ensured the door-locks would not fasten.

When the King heard the noise of the band of would-be murderers trying to get in, he quickly tore up the floorboards and hid in a vault below.

One of the ladies with him, Katherine Douglas, is said to have put her arm through the staples of the room-door to prevent Graham's band bursting in, but to no avail. Ultimately, the King was discovered, and stabbed to death.

There was a cruel sequel. The Queen—and the King's great love— was Lady Joan Beaufort, daughter of the Earl of Somerset. He had fallen in love with her when he was in England, and wrote beautiful poetry about her, and called her his "milk-white dove".

She was grief-stricken at James' murder, and vowed never to rest until the killers were caught.

Their end was terrible. The conspirators were tortured for three days. Graham was nailed naked to a tree and dragged through the streets. He was tortured with red-hot pincers. His son was also tortured in front of him and then executed on the Heading Hill of the Gowan Hills.

Atholl—thought to be plotting to succeed to the throne—had a crown of red-hot metal placed on his head and was not executed at the Heading Hill, but died after torture. Eventually, Graham, too, had his agonies ended by the headsman's axe. Violent days!

There are light-hearted memories, too, of the Gowan Hills.

One section, at the north end, was known as Hurly-Hawky, well-known as the site of a sliding game, using the skeleton of a cow's head as a kind of sledge. The name is said to derive from the words hurl, to move rapidly, and hawky, a name for a cow.

King James V—the "Gudeman of Ballengeich"—is believed to have taken part in this amusement, sometimes repeated today by children using pieces of old carpet or linoleum as sledges.

Tolbooth tales

A glance at the list of inmates within the jails of yesteryear proves that violence and lawbreaking are not peculiar to the twenty-first century.

In October 1841 the county jail, next to Stirling Tolbooth, was bursting with thieves, eight embezzlers and designers of fraudulent schemes, two child murderers, and thirteen house-breakers. Others had been found guilty of culpable homicide, assault, desertion, forgery, prison breaking, malicious mischief, poaching and one for concealment of pregnancy.

Folks were also locked up in the Tolbooth itself, by the town council, for a variety of reasons. Two fellows who'd been found guilty by the Kirk Sessions of playing dice until 4 a.m. were confined there for some time on a diet of bread and water, that was in 1598.

In June, 1724, Francis Hunter found himself 'doing porridge' after welshing on a debt to Margaret Clark, the local washer-wife. The sentence was that he would remain there until he paid her 38 shillings (£1.90) 'for washing and mending of his cloaths'.

But there was compassion where necessary. Janet Connochie was given a regular supply of coal while a prisoner as her child was staying with her during the sentence.

Of course serious offences meant the death penalty and the hangman was an important citizen. He got ten shillings a week (50 pence) plus numerous perks. A whipping through the town brought in a bonus of 13s 4d (about 70 pence) and an execution paid £4. On top of that he got a rent free home, coat for nothing, a suit of clothes, and a supply of grain from all farmers who attended the market.

Whipped through Stirling

Punishment of criminals in yesteryear Stirling was strange. Folk who got drunk, hit the wife or started a punch-up with their neighbour were likely to be sentenced to a public whipping through every street in town!

A crowd of 5,000 turned out to watch the last whipping on July 2, 1830. The 'victims', if that is the correct word, were two well-known troublemakers named Ord and McKenzie. They had committed serious assaults and been found guilty before the Sheriff-Deputy of Stirlingshire at an earlier court hearing.

Officials, fearing that the crowd might get carried away with the excitement of the occasion, took the precaution of swearing in 100 special constables. The whipping began at 2 p.m. when Ord and McKenzie were tied to a cart. They received a total of 36 lashes each.

Another memorable occasion when the public could see justice being done at first hand was in 1848. In that year the full pomp of the provost, magistrates, and high constables was mustered in Broad Street to officially 'drum out' a gang of prostitutes!

The bodysnatchers

In the earlier years of the nineteenth century doctors found it very difficult to get bodies for research because of the public's attitude to human dissection, so they gladly paid out huge sums of money to folk who could keep them supplied.

Most corpses found their way to the anatomist's table after being stolen from the grave and the medical men, usually folk of high principle, never asked any questions.

A dark cloudy night with no moon or an evening of torrential rain were ideal conditions for the bodysnatchers or 'Resurrectionists" as these traders in human corpses were known.

In 1822 the beadle of Stirling's West Church noticed one morning that the grave of a woman called Witherspoon had been disturbed. Later Bailie Jaffrey, who had a grocery store in Baker Street, gave orders that the grave was to be opened. The body had vanished from the coffin and the shroud and dead-clothes were huddled together at one end of the grave.

They received a total of 36 lashes each

No-one was ever caught for this outrage, but at the Spring Circuit Court of 1822 a grave-digger and some others were tried on a charge of lifting bodies from Stirling Churchyard. They claimed the orders to steal the bodies had been given by a doctor but he left the town before proceedings could be taken against him.

The citizens, bitter about the activities of the despicable body-snatchers, rioted during the trial and the 77th Regiment had to be drafted in to calm the mob. They fired over the heads of the crowd. No-one was injured.

To counter the activities of Ressurectionists, who were seldom caught, families had their nearest and dearest buried with an iron cage secured around the coffin. This was kept there until the body was past being of use to doctors.

However it was only when the law made provision for medics to be supplied with specimens that the problem was finally eased.

Wolf on the crag

A wolf once saved Stirling from destruction and the townsfolk from certain death. In the ninth century two Northumbrian princes, named Osbrecht and Ella, seized much of East and Central Scotland from Donald V, King of Scots. Stirling was one of their strongholds and was guarded by scores of soldiers.

But soon they were under attack and efforts were made to take the town from them just as they had seized it from the Scots. I use the word town but of course in those times Stirling was a village of just a few hundred inhabitants who lived in wooden houses built beside the fortress. Nevertheless this was an important place and our two Northumbrian princes did all they could to protect it from a threatened invasion by the Danes who had earlier brought terror to many towns in Britain.

At a crag on the southern side of town a sentry was posted to keep watch round the clock.But one of the soldiers involved in this task fell asleep on duty - on the very night that the enemy was poised to attack.

In that fascinating old book *The Stirling Repository* we are told: 'The besieging foe was at hand, and was about to take the city, when a wolf, alarmed at the noise and din of the advancing hordes crept for safety to the

A dark night with no moon was an ideal time for plying this unspeakable trade

The wolf's cry saved the town

crag on which the sleeping soldier lay.

'But still he found no safety. He growled in terror. It was his wild cry that saved the city. It awoke the sleeping sentinel, who, seeing the position of matters, raised the alarm.

'He was not yet too late. The citizens arose, buckled on their armour, and drove the Danes from the district, thus the wolf saved the city.'

Later the seal of the burgh became a wolf recumbent on a crag and those who asked about the origin of the design were told this story.

Facts do exist to back up the yarn. For a start wolves were reported in the area. In 1288 the accounts record an allowance 'for two park-keepers and one hunter of wolves at Stirling'.

The glowing hand

King Robert the Bruce knew that he would win the battle of Bannockburn in 1314 - before the fighting had even started! And it was all thanks to a phantom monk.

Robert had ordered a priest to bring the glowing hand of the holy Saint Fillan from Stirling Castle to the battlefield. The Lord had made the hand give off bright light so that Saint Fillan could work long into the night while writing out the Holy Scriptures.

The king was convinced that the presence of the hand would bring Scotland good luck in the confrontation that lay ahead. However the priest, fearing that the hand might be lost to the English, hid it in one of the castle dungeons and brought the empty box to Bannockburn. He anticipated that Robert wouldn't ask to see inside, but he was wrong.

'Let me look at the hand,' said his king and, trembling with fear the priest slowly lifted the top off. By a miracle the glowing hand was inside. However, standing opposite, and only visible to the priest, was a stern faced monk dressed in a long white gown. He warned the Royal messenger: 'Never again must you disobey your King.'

The father broke down and confessed all to Robert. He expected to be cruelly punished for disobeying such an important order but the king simply smiled and said a short prayer, for he knew this was an omen that his side would score an important victory in the fighting. And, of course, Scotland were indeed victorious at Bannockburn.

Loch Lomond's story

by John Mackay

After it was shaped by the primeval forces, colossal glaciers of the Ice Age moved across the land we know as Scotland and ground their way between the granite heights, to form deep fissures on the country's face, one of them 24 miles long.

And when the warmer airs of later years arrived, this fissure filled with the melting ice and made a loch some 700 feet deep in one place, becoming the largest of our freshwater lochs and the largest inland water in Britain. Through ensuing centuries a splendour of woodland growth, of heather and bracken and of surrounding land, well cultivated, made it a scenic wonderland, known to us today as Loch Lomond.

The most famous of Scotland's lochs was not named until the thirteenth century when it took its title from the Ben rising 3,192 feet on its eastward side. The Ben had been called after Laomain, a legendary hero of the Celts.

The whole district is however sometimes called 'The Lennox' derived from 'Levenax' the name first given to the river flowing out of the southern end of the loch (now 'Leven') - a name associated with one of the great familes of Scotland - the Earls of Lennox of the Macfarlane clan.

Much on the early story of Loch Lomond is traditional. One such, that the waters have risen in the last three hundred years, for tales have come about of former dwellers on the lochside swearing to have seen in certain lights, houses and an orchard underwater.

And there is a triple saying associated with the loch, that it has - 'Waves without wind' - 'Fish without fins' - 'Islands that float'.

Of the first of these three, this is possible, since long after a storm has passed, a swell at its widest southern end can continue to agitate the waters. Fish without fins could be eels; or snakes in the old days.

Islands may well have 'floated' in the shape of crannogs - the lake dwellings of prehistoric times, a kind of raft built on stilts driven into the loch bed.

These lake dwellers lived secure from attack from the land and with the knowledge that they were also immune in an inland water from attacks from the sea.

As well that they had not lived in such a way there some centuries on, for Loch Lomond now comes into recorded history in the early thirteenth century when Magnus, King of the Isle of Man, son-in-law of Viking Haco sailed his sixty longships up the sea waters of Loch Long to where Arrochar now stands and proceeded to have some of his longships dragged across land to the narrows of Loch Lomond from where they sailed down, pillaging the shore dwellings - 'their sea-boats creating as much astonishment in Lennox as if they had fallen from the sky'.

Early in the next century Robert the Bruce in his guerrilla-war days used what is now known as Rob Roy's cave above the shore near Inversnaid and is also said to have caused yew trees to be planted on one or two islands of the loch to be fashioned in future into bows for Scotland's warrior archers.

The clan feuds

Clans were, by then, settled around the shores. The Colquhouns to the west, who traced their ancestry back to the twelfth century. Northwards, the Macfarlanes of the ancient Lennox line; and Alpin who reigned over part of Scotland in the eighth century.

Throughout the following years a succession of feuds with those fighting clans culminated at the beginning of the seventeenth century with the bloodiest of all battles between the Colquhouns against the MacGregors, near Rossdhu, ancestral home of the Colquhouns.

It was a comparatively slight incident which sparked off the conflict. Two MacGregors, returning on foot from the Lowlands, asked for refreshment at the Colquhoun house. Contrary to accepted rules of Highland hospitality, this was refused and the two hungry clansmen were sent on their way - but stopped when out of sight, to kill one of the Colquhoun sheep.

Part of the carcass was royally roasted and eaten round a woodland fire, the smoke of which attracted the attention of those at Rossdhu. A band of the Colquhouns crept up on the two at their feast, and without further ado, hauled them away to their execution for theft.

When word got through to Inversnaid, the MacGregor revenge was terrible. They came down on the Colquhouns joining in battle by Glen Fruin west of Rossdhu.

Sir Walter Scott wrote on the conflict:

The Viking raid!

'Proudly our pibroch has thrilled in Glen Fruin,
And Bannacha's groans to our slogan replied;
Glen Luss and Rossdhu they are smoking in ruin;
And the best of Loch Lomond lie dead on its side.
Widow and Saxon maid
Long shall lament our raid
Think of Clan Alpin with fear and with woe...'

Within days, a macabre procession set out for Stirling where the Court was in residence.

Escorted by armed clansmen against any further surprise attack the widows of the slain Colquhouns all clothed in black and mounted on white horses, each carrying their husband's bloodstained shirts before them, arrived in this manner to plead with King James VI for vengeance.

The MacGregors, for long a thorn in the flesh of the monarchy, were outlawed. For some ensuing years this clan suffered the indignity of being 'nameless' and 'landless'. But such a powerful body of men were deemed better as friends than as lawless enemies by succeeding rulers and towards the end of the seventeenth century the MacGregors were pardoned and their ancient rights restored.

Not that this was the end of their troubles with authority for in 1671 there was born a man who was destined to be outlawed with his men once again, before becoming, as chief of the clan, almost unbelievably, a Highland constable to enforce law and order - a man of contradictions - Rob Roy MacGregor himself.

When Rob was still a babe in arms, a chief of his clan died in his farmhouse at the head of Loch Lomond and it is interesting to note the still pagan style of burial observed in these days - 'a curious mixture of Celtic pageantry and the Presbyterian service'.

The burial took place on the island of Inchcailloch where the pipers played a lament, slowly pacing 'while the Hereditary Bard chanted the departed chiefs pedigree through thirty generations and more back to king Alpin'.

There are thirty islands on the loch. Today, Inchcailloch boasts one of the finest examples of a natural oak wood and has been chosen as the Loch Lomond Nature Reserve. In ancient times it was known as 'the island of women' it being then, the site of a nunnery. And it had a male counterpart in the island of Inchtavvanach, once a monastery.

Deer parks have been at times established on the larger islands -

notably on Inchmurrin, the largest of them all, which now has farmland - much changed from the days when the Earls of Lennox built their castle on this island fastness.

Cattle rustlers

Traffic in the Highlands in these wild days (apart from marauding bands of pursuing redcoats in the Jacobite Risings) was mainly the movement of cattle - the wide-horned shaggy beasts, beef on the hoof, which were the material wealth of many a chief.

At certain times of the year herds were driven south for sale at the markets, along the 'drove roads' - not roads at all, but tracks worn through the years by the passage of cattle. Weather apart, all should have been a simple enough operation for that tough body of men, the drovers, but cattle rustling in Scotland preceded that portrayed in the cinema of the Wild West by many years!

It was John Campbell, first Earl of Breadalbane who put forward a scheme that a 'Captain of the Watch' should be responsible for keeping the peace along the Highland Line and discourage rustlers.

Unbelievably to some, Rob Roy was appointed to the post.

Whatever the wisdom or otherwise of the appointment, it was impressive enough for the chief of the Colquhouns to forget the feuds with the MacGregors and lace his herds under Rob's protection. The two met on the island of Inchlonaig out from Rossdhu Priory (where, incidentally, Sir Walter Scott stayed while working on his novel *Rob Roy*) and signed a contract.

In some ways, with the advent of the Captain of the Watch, another modern term might be said to have meaning in these days of the eighteenth century: the 'protection racket'. And it worked in devious ways. Here are two instances.

If a body of rustlers were caught, but could convince Rob Roy that the stolen cattle were not under his, Rob Roy's, protection, they were allowed to pass through the MacGregor country on Loch Lomondside - providing they gave over a small share of the spoils.

One of the drove roads went along the shore of the loch by the Pass of Balmaha and into the MacGregor lands. These roads as already mentioned, were more like 'tree-clad mountainsides' and in the following situation, a mettlesome old bull, the leader of the herd even found the going so hard (they were not going to the market but going north) that by the time they reached Rowardennan 'a child might have scratched his ears'.

This particular happening was an example of the individual way the MacGregors had of looking at the job, for they were returning with a herd 'taken' from one of Rob's customers who had been tardy in paying his protection money!

Inversnaid, at the heart of the MacGregor country northwards on Loch Lomond, figured in many of the clan ploys; and when the government decided in the early 1700s to build a fort there to control these Highlanders who were too often a law unto themselves, the MacGregors bided their time...

A Mr. Nasmyth from Edinburgh, builder of the fort, left a Stirling hostelry one winter's day and rode to Inversnaid to check if all had been completed in the time agreed with the military. Happily this was so, and his workmen, relieved to have the construction finished and now keen to return home, lit a good fire and settled down for the night against their departure next morning.

In the late evening a weak hammering at the gate of the fort was found to be made by an exhausted traveller who had lost his way and craved shelter. The gate was opened - and in rushed a band of the MacGregors armed for a fight which proved unnecessary, for Nasmyth and his men were only glad enough to be spared as they were driven out into the inhospitable dark to find their blundering way back to the kinder Lowlands. The MacGregors then blew one wall down with gunpowder and made a bonfire of the furniture within, which 'lit Glen Arklet from end to end'.

Many of the stories associated with Rob Roy and Loch Lomond have been made up by writers more interested in a good story then in the truth. Even Sir Walter Scott is at times inclined to liven up truth with his special brand of fiction to stir the imagination and improve on what might be termed the original. In some instances he had to do his best when a story intrigued but had little reference to help him in his retelling.

And the following piratical adventure, although written of by Sir Walter in later pages of this book, has been thought worth enlarging upon after discovering further factual evidence of the occasion in a government pamphlet of the time.

The loch pirates

In the earlier Jacobite Risings the clans around the loch were, in general, for the Stuart cause; and the MacGregors, well aware that their lands around Glen Arklet would be easily open to attack by water should the government troops sail up the loch and land in force on the shore by Inversnaid, decided to take away all available craft on the loch and leave the enemy without means of such an approach.

About seventy of the younger clansmen launched their own modest collection of boats and rowed down the loch to Inchmurrin. They waited there until midnight; then ventured out and into all the bays between Balmaha and Rossdhu and along each shoreland, pulling out every kind of boat and towing them away across the moonlit water.

By morning, they were back at Inchmurrin with their newly won fleet. They rested there all day, then rowed back up the loch at night and hid their boats and their stolen craft under the bushes and tall heather clumps by the shore. Then exhausted with this unaccustomed exercise, being more at home on land, they went their weary way back to join the MacGregors at their inland camp.

But the alarm had been raised. Rob's men had bargained without the navy who supplied eight boats with guns mounted which were towed up the Leven by teams of horses.

A contingent of volunteers from Dumbarton joined their opposite number from Glasgow. All stayed that night at Luss from where the whole armed assembly embarked next morning and came at noon by Inversnaid.

'As a precaution, a ball was fired through the roof of a house on to the face of the mountain, whereupon an old wife or two came crawling out... The Lowland volunteers with the greatest intrepidity leap'd on shore.... drew up in order and stood about an hour, their ner drums beating all the while'.

The stolen boats were found and 'hurled' down to the water 'and all dropped down to Luss that same evening... the naval guns and the muskets of the volunteers were discharged into the air' (as they sailed down) 'and made so very dreadful a Noise that the MacGregors were cowed and frightened away'.

Thus ended a surely non-event with the government pamphlet guilty of a touch of fiction too and the truth of it may well he that at least on the government side, the volunteers after making some show of strength, had

The MacGregors' 'piracy' of enemy craft

shot their muskets into the air in an expression of joyous relief that they had not been required to meet these terrible Highlanders.

The last Jacobite Rising of 1745 is also connected with Loch Lomond, but in a very different way: the world famous song 'The Bonny Banks o' Loch Lomond' has these oft quoted words:

> *'O, ye'll tak' the high road,*
> *And I'll tak' the low road*
> *And I'll be in Scotland afore ye..."*

These words are said to have been spoken before his execution in Carlisle by a Jacobite soldier to his sweetheart who had walked all the way from Loch Lomondside to see him for the last time: the 'high road' meaning her way back to Scotland - the 'low road' his way to the grave: and 'I'll be in Scotland afore ye', meaning that on his death, his liberated spirit would immediately return to the scene of their plighted troth.

This is only one explanation of the puzzling words. In another version, there is no question of executions and the like; a more optimistic note is struck singing:

> *'We'll meet where we parted in bonny Luss Glen,*
> *'mang the heathery braes o' Loch Lomond'.*

The Trossachs

The origin of the name Trossachs and the exact area of land that this term covers often confuses folk. Some experts say that it means 'bristled territory' whilst others say the name refers to 'The Cross Places' - an allusion to the way the glens run perhaps?

The Trossachs in the proper sense of the word is an area of unrivalled beauty extending to little more than one square mile between Loch Achray and Loch Katrine. This tree-filled valley contains some of the most varied scenery to be found in Scotland.

But a much wider area - from Loch Earn in the north to the Lake of Menteith in the south and from Doune in the east to Loch Lomond in the west - is generally regarded as being the Trossachs.

The main town of the Trossachs is Callander which was made even more famous as Tannochbrae in the BBC TV series *Dr. Finlay's Casebook.*

In times past it was a favourite meeting place for drovers, bringing their cattle from the hills to the markets of Central Scotland.

Ben Ledi stands majestically at 2,874 feet overlooking the town and nearby we can see the narrow Pass and Falls of Leny where Highlanders once hid amongst the trees and defied the redcoats.

Beyond the Pass of Leny is Loch Lubnaig into the head of which, from Strathyre and Balquhidder, flows the Balvaig River. It was here that Rob Roy succeeded in escaping when a prisoner in the hands of the Duke of Montrose. Laggan Farm is said to be the birthplace of Rob's wife and far up the glen lies Inverlochlarig Farm where he eventually died.

North of Strathyre on the west shore of Loch Earn is Lochearnhead, a popular centre for sailing and water ski-ing holidays.

No visit would be complete without a stroll round the picturesque village of Aberfoyle - now a far far cry from the 'Clachan' of Sir Walter Scott's works.

It was here that Bailie Nicol Jarvie and Frank Osbaldistone journeyed from Glasgow to meet Rob Roy.

Nearby is Loch Ard - some say this spectacular stretch of water is the jewel of the Trossachs. It is three miles long and a half mile wide and is dominated on the west by Ben Lomond.

Adventures of Rob Roy

by Sir Walter Scott

Rob Roy MacGregor Campbell, which last name he bore in consequence of the acts of Parliament abolishing his own, was the youngest son of Donald MacGregor of Glengyle, said to have been a Lieutenant-Colonel (probably in the service of James II) by his wife, a daughter of Campbell of Glenfalloch.

Rob's own designation was of Inversnaid; but he appears to have acquired a right of some kind or other to the property or possession of Craig Royston, a domain of rock and forest, lying on the east side of Loch Lomond, where that beautiful lake stretches into the dusky mountains of Glenfalloch.

The time of his birth is uncertain. But he is said to have been active in the scenes of war and plunder which succeeded the Revolution; and tradition affirms him to have been the leader in a predatory incursion into the parish of Kippen, in the Lennox, which took place in the year 1691.

It was of almost a bloodless character, only one person losing his life; but from the extent of the depredation, it was long distinguished by the name of the Her'-ship, or devastation, of Kippen.

The time of his death is also uncertain; but as he is said to have survived the year 1733, and died an aged man, it is probable he may have been twenty-five about the time of the Her'-ship of Kippen, which would assign his birth to the middle of the seventeenth century.

In the more quiet times which succeeded the Revolution, Rob Roy, or Red Robert, seems to have exerted his active talents, which were of no mean order, as a drover, or trader in cattle, to a great extent.

It may well be supposed that in those days no Lowland, much less English drovers, ventured to enter the Highlands. The cattle, which were the staple commodity of the mountains, were escorted down to fairs, on the borders of the Lowlands, by a party of Highlanders, with their arms rattling around them; and who dealt, however, in all honour and good faith with their Southern customers.

A fray, indeed, would sometimes arise when the Lowlandmen, chiefly Borderers, who had to supply the English market, used to dip their bonnets in the next brook, and wrapping them round their hands, oppose their cudgels to the naked broadswords, which had not always the superiority.

The Lowlandmen would oppose their cudgels to the naked broadswords

I have heard from aged persons, who had been engaged in such affrays, that the Highlanders used remarkably fair play, never using the point of their sword, far less their pistols or daggers; so that

'With many a stiff thwack and many a bang.
Hard crabtree and cold iron rang.'

A slash or two, or a broken head, was easily accommodated, and as the trade was of benefit to both parties, trifling skirmishes were not allowed to interrupt its harmony.

Indeed, it was of vital interest to the Highlanders, whose income, so far as derived from their estates, depended entirely on the sale of black cattle; and a sagacious and experienced dealer benefited not only himself, but his friends and neighbours, by his speculations.

Those of Rob Roy were for several years so successful as to inspire general confidence, and raise him in the estimation of the country in which he resided.

His importance was increased by the death of his father, in consequence of which he succeeded to the management of his nephew Gregor MacGregor of Glengyle's property, and, as his tutor, to such influence with the clan and following as was due to the representative of Dougal Ciar.

Such influence was the more uncontrolled, that this family of the MacGregors seem to have refused adherence to MacGregor of Glencarnock, and asserted a kind of independence.

It was at this time that Rob Roy acquired an interest by purchase, wadset, or otherwise, to the property of Craig Royston. He was in particular favour, during this prosperous period of his life, with his nearest and most powerful neighbour, James first Duke of Montrose, from whom he received many marks of regard.

His Grace consented to give his nephew and himself a right of property on the estates of Glengyle and Inversnaid, which they had till then only held as kindly tenants.

The Duke, also, with a view to the interest of the country and his own estate, supported our adventurer by loans of money to a considerable amount, to enable him to carry on his speculations in the cattle trade.

Unfortunately that species of commerce was and is liable to sudden fluctuations; and Rob Roy was - by a sudden depression of markets, and as a friendly tradition adds, by the bad faith of a partner named Macdonald, whom he had imprudently received into his confidence, and intrusted with a considerable sum of money - rendered totally insolvent.

He absconded, of course - not empty handed, if it be true, as stated in an advertisement for his apprehension, that he had in his possession sums to the amount of £1,000 sterling, obtained from several noblemen and gentlemen under pretence of purchasing cows for them in the Highlands.

This advertisement appeared in June 1712, and was several times repeated. It fixes the period when Rob Roy exchanged his commercial adventures for speculations of a very different complexion.

He appears at this period first to have removed from his ordinary dwelling at Inversnaid, ten or twelve Scots miles (which is double the number of English) farther into the Highlands, and commenced the lawless sort of life which he afterwards followed.

The Duke of Montrose, who conceived himself deceived and cheated by MacGregor's conduct, employed legal means to recover the money lent to him. Rob Roy's landed property was attached by the regular form of legal procedure, and his stock and furniture made the subject of arrest and sale.

It is said that this diligence of the law, as it is called in Scotland, which the English more bluntly term distress, was used in this case with uncommon severity, and that the legal satellites, not usually the gentlest persons in the world, had insulted MacGregor's wife, in a manner which would have aroused a milder man than he to thoughts of unbounded vengeance.

She was a woman of fierce and haughty temper, and is not unlikely to have disturbed the officers in the execution of their duty, and thus to have incurred ill-treatment, though, for the sake of humanity, it is hoped that the story sometimes told is a popular exaggeration.

It is certain that she felt extreme anguish at being expelled from the banks of Loch Lomond, and gave vent to her feelings in a fine piece of pipe-music, still well known to amateurs by the name of 'Rob Roy's Lament'.

The fugitive is thought to have found his first place of refuge in Glen Dochart, under the Earl of Breadalbane's protection; for though that family had been active agents in the destruction of the MacGregors in former times, they had of late sheltered a great many of the name in their old possessions.

The Duke of Argyll was also one of Rob Roy's protectors, so far as to afford him, according to the Highland phrase, wood and water - the shelter, namely, that is afforded by the forests and lakes of an inaccessible country.

The great men of the Highlands in that time, besides being anxious-

The Lawmen had insulted Rob's wife

ly ambitious to keep up what was called their Following, or military retainers, were also desirous to have at their disposal men of resolute character, to whom the world and the world's law were no friends, and who might at times ravage the lands or destroy the tenants of a feudal enemy, without bringing responsibility on their patrons.

The strife between the names of Campbell and Graham, during the civil wars of the seventeenth century, had been stamped with mutual loss and inveterate enmity.

The death of the great Marquess of Montrose on the one side, the defeat at Inverlochy, and cruel plundering of Lorn, on the other, were reciprocal injuries not likely to be forgotten.

Rob Roy was therefore sure of refuge in the country of the Campbells, both as having assumed their name, as connected by his mother with the family of Glenfalloch, and as an enemy to the rival house of Montrose.

The extent of Argyll's possessions, and the power of retreating thither in any emergency, gave great encouragement to the bold schemes of revenge which he had adopted.

This was nothing short of the maintenance of a predatory war against the Duke of Montrose, whom he considered as the author of his exclusion from civil society, and of the outlawry to which he had been sentenced by letters of horning and caption (legal writs so called), as well as the seizure of his goods, and adjudication of his landed property.

Against his Grace, therefore, his tenants, friends, allies, and relatives, he disposed himself to employ every means of annoyance in his power; and though this was a circle sufficiently extensive for active depredation, Rob, who professed himself a Jacobite, took the liberty of extending his sphere of operations against all whom he chose to consider as friendly to the revolutionary government, or to that most obnoxious of measures - the Union of the Kingdoms.

Under one or other of these pretexts all his neighbours of the Lowlands who had anything to lose, or were unwilling to compound for security by paying him an annual sum for protection or forbearance, were exposed to his ravages.

The country in which this private warfare or system of depredation was to be carried on was, until opened up by roads, in the highest degree favourable for his purpose.

It was broken up into narrow valleys, the habitable part of which bore no proportion to the huge wildernesses of forest, rocks, and precipices by which they were encircled, and which was, moreover, full of inextricable passes, morasses, and natural strengths, unknown to any but the inhabitants themselves, where a few men acquainted with the ground were capable, with ordinary address, of baffling the pursuit of numbers.

The opinions and habits of the nearest neighbours to the Highland line were also highly favourable to Rob Roy's purpose.

A large proportion of them were of his own clan of MacGregor, who claimed the property of Balquhidder, and other Highland districts, as having been part of the ancient possessions of their tribe; though the harsh laws, under the severity of which they had suffered so deeply, had assigned the ownership to other families.

The civil wars of the seventeenth century had accustomed these men to the use of arms, and they were peculiarly brave and fierce from remembrance of their sufferings.

The vicinity of a comparatively rich Lowland district gave also great temptations to incursion. Many belonging to other clans, habituated to contempt of industry and to the use of arms, drew towards an unprotected frontier which promised facility of plunder; and the state of the country, now so peaceable and quiet, verified at that time the opinion which Dr. Johnson heard with doubt and suspicion, that the most disorderly and lawless districts of the Highlands were those which lay nearest to the Lowland line.

There was therefore no difficulty in Rob Roy, descended of a tribe which was widely dispersed in the country we have described, collecting any number of followers whom he might be able to keep in action, and to maintain by his proposed operations.

He himself appears to have been singularly adapted for the profession which he proposed to exercise. His stature was not of the tallest, but his person was uncommonly strong and compact.

The greatest peculiarities of his frame were the breadth of his shoulders, and the great and almost dis-proportioned length of his arms; so remarkable, indeed, that it was said he could, without stooping, tie the garters of his Highland hose, which are placed two inches below the knee.

His countenance was open, manly, stern at periods of danger, but frank and cheerful in his hours of festivity.

His hair was dark-red, thick and frizzled, and curled short around the face. His fashion of dress showed, of course, the knees and upper part of the leg, which was described to me as resembling that of a Highland bull, hirsute, with red hair, and evincing muscular strength similar to that animal.

To these personal qualifications must be added a masterly use of the Highland sword, in which his length of arm gave him great advantage - and a perfect and intimate knowledge of all the recesses of the wild country in which he harboured, and the character of the various individuals, whether friendly or hostile, with whom he might come in contact.

His mental qualities seem to have been no less adapted to the circumstances in which he was placed. Though the descendant of the bloodthirsty Ciar Mohr, he inherited none of his ancestor's ferocity.

On the contrary, Rob Roy avoided every appearance of cruelty, and it is not averred that he was ever the means of unnecessary bloodshed, or the actor in any deed which could lead the way to it.

His schemes of plunder were contrived and executed with equal boldness and sagacity, and were almost universally successful, from the skill with which they were laid, and the secrecy and rapidity with which they were executed.

Like Robin Hood of England, he was a kind and gentle robber, and, while he took from the rich, was liberal in relieving the poor.

All whom I have conversed with, and I have in my youth seen some who knew Rob Roy personally, gave him the character of a benevolent and humane man.

His ideas of morality were those of an Arab chief, being such as naturally arose out of his wild education. Supposing Rob Roy to have argued on the tendency of the life which he pursued, whether from choice or from necessity, he would doubtless have assumed to himself the character of a brave man, who, deprived of his natural rights by the partiality of laws, endeavoured to assert them by the strong hand of natural power... We are not, however, to suppose the character of this distinguished outlaw to be that of an actual hero, acting uniformly and consistently on such moral principles as the illustrious bard who, standing by his grave, has vindicated his fame. (Wordsworth: *Rob Roy's Grave*.)

On the contrary, as is common with barbarous chiefs, Rob Roy appears to have mixed his professions of principle with a large alloy of craft and dis-simulation, of which his conduct during the civil war is sufficient proof.

It is also said, and truly, that although his courtesy was one of his strongest characteristics, yet sometimes he assumed an arrogance of manner which was not easily endured by the high-spirited men to whom it was addressed, and drew the daring outlaw into frequent disputes, from which he did not always come off with credit.

From this it has been inferred that Rob Roy was more of a bully than a hero, or at least that he had, according to the common phrase, his fighting days.

Some aged men who knew him well have described him also as better at a *taich-tulzie*, or scuffle within doors, than in mortal combat.

The tenor of his life may be quoted to repel this charge; while at the same time it must be allowed, that the situation in which he was placed rendered him prudently averse to maintaining quarrels, where nothing was to be had save blows, and where success would have raised up against him new and powerful enemies, in a country where revenge was still considered as a duty rather than a crime.

The power of commanding his passions on such occasions, far from being inconsistent with the part which MacGregor had to perform, was essentially necessary, at the period when he lived, to prevent his career from being cut short...

Occasionally Rob Roy suffered disasters, and incurred great personal danger.

On one remarkable occasion he was saved by the coolness of his lieutenant, Macanaleister, or Fletcher, the Little John of his band - a fine active fellow, of course, and celebrated as a marksman.

It happened that MacGregor and his party had been surprised and dispersed by a superior force of horse and foot. and the word was given to 'split and squander'.

Each shifted for himself, but a bold dragoon attached himself to pursuit of Rob, and overtaking him, struck at him with his broadsword. A plate of iron in his bonnet saved MacGregor from being cut down to the teeth; but the blow was heavy enough to bear him to the ground, crying, as he fell, 'O, Macanaleister, is there naething in her?' (i.e. the gun).

The trooper, at the same time, exclaiming, 'Damn ye, your mother never wrought your nightcap!' had his arm raised for a second blow, when Macanaleister fired, and the ball pierced the dragoon's heart.

Such as he was, Rob Roy's progress in his occupation is thus described by a gentleman of sense and talent, who resided within the circle of his predatory wars, had probably felt their effects, and speaks of them, as might be expected, with little of the forbearance with which, from their peculiar and romantic character, they are now regarded.

The ball pierced the dragoon's heart

'This man (Rob Roy MacGregor) was a person of sagacity, and neither wanted stratagem nor address; and, having abandoned himself to all licentiousness, set himself at the head of all the loose, vagrant, and desperate people of that clan, in the west end of Perth and Stirlingshires, and infested those whole countries with thefts, robberies, and depredations.

Very few who lived within his reach (that is, within the distance of a nocturnal expedition) could promise to themselves security, either for their persons or effects, without subjecting themselves to pay him a heavy and shameful tax of black-mail.

He at last proceeded to such a degree of audaciousness, that he committed robberies, raised contributions, and resented quarrels, at the head of a very considerable body of armed men, in open day, and in the face of the Government.'

The extent and success of these depredations cannot be surprising, when we consider that the scene of them was laid in a country where the general law was neither enforced nor respected.

The period of the Rebellion, 1715, approached soon after Rob Roy had attained celebrity. His Jacobite partialities were now placed in opposition to his sense of the obligations which he owed to the indirect protection of the Duke of Argyll.

But the desire of 'drowning his sounding steps amid the din of general war', induced him to join the forces of the Earl of Mar, although his patron, the Duke of Argyll, was at the head of the army opposed to the Highland insurgents.

The MacGregors - a large sept of them at least, that of Ciar Mohr - on this occasion were not commanded by Rob Roy, but by his nephew, Gregor MacGregor, otherwise called James Grahame of Glengyle, and still better remembered by the Gaelic epithet of *Ghlune Dhu*, i.e., Black Knee, from a black spot on one of his knees, which his Highland garb rendered visible.

There can be no question, however, that being then very young, Glengyle must have acted on most occasions by the advice and direction of so experienced a leader as his uncle.

The MacGregors assembled in numbers at that period, and began even to threaten the Lowlands towards the lower extremity of Loch Lomond.

They suddenly seized all the boats which were upon the loch, and, probably with a view to some enterprise of their own, drew them overland to Inversnaid, in order to intercept the progress of a large body of west-country whigs who were in arms for the Government, and moving in that direction.

The whigs made an excursion for the recovery of the boats. Their forces consisted of volunteers from Paisley, Kilpatrick, and elsewhere, who, with the assistance of a body of seamen, were towed up the river Leven in longboats belonging to the ships of war then lying in the Clyde.

At Luss they were joined by the forces of Sir Humphrey Colquhoun, and James Grant, his son-in-law, with their followers, attired in the Highland dress of the period, which is picturesquely described.

The whole party crossed to Craig-Royston, but the MacGregors did not offer combat.

If we are to believe the account of the expedition given by the historian Rae, they leaped on shore at Craig-Royston with the utmost intrepidity, no enemy appearing to oppose them, and, by the noise of their drums, which they beat incessantly, and the discharge of their artillery and small arms, terrified the MacGregors, whom they appear never to have seen, out of their fastnesses, and caused them to fly in a panic to the general camp of the Highlanders at Strath Fillan.

The low-country men succeeded in getting possession of the boats, at a great expenditure of noise and courage, and little risk.

After this temporary removal from his old haunts, Rob Roy was sent by the Earl of Mar to Aberdeen, to raise, it is believed, a part of the clan Gregor which is settled in that country.

These men were of his own family (the race of the Ciar Mohr). They were the descendants of about three hundred MacGregors whom the Earl of Murray, about the year 1624, transported from his estates in Monteith to oppose his enemies the Macintoshes, a race as hardy and restless as they were themselves.

But while in the city of Aberdeen Rob Roy met a relation of a very different class and character from those whom he was sent to summon to arms. This was Dr. James Gregory (by descent a MacGregor), the patriarch of a dynasty of professors distinguished for literary and scientific talent, and the grandfather of the late eniment physician and accomplished scholar, Professor Gregory of Edinburgh.

This gentleman was at the time Professor of Medicine in King's College, Aberdeen, and son of Dr. James Gregory, distinguished in science as the inventor of the reflecting telescope.

With such a family it may seem our friend Rob could have had little in common. But civil war is a species of misery which introduces men to strange bedfellows.

Dr. Gregory thought it a point of prudence to claim kindred, at so critical a period, with a man so formidable and influential.

He invited Rob Roy to his house, and treated him with so much kindness, that he produced in his generous bosom a degree of gratitude which seemed likely to occasion very inconvenient effects.

The Professor had a son about eight or nine years old - a lively, stout boy - with whose appearance our Highland Robin Hood was much taken.

On the day before his departure from the house of his learned relative, Rob Roy, who had pondered deeply how he might requite his cousin's kindness, took Dr. Gregory aside, and addressed him to this purpose: 'My dear kinsman, I have been thinking what I could do to show my sense of your hospitality.

'Now, here you have a fine spirited son, whom you are ruining by cramming him with your useless book-learning, and I am determined, by way of manifesting my great good-will to you and yours, to take him with me and make a man of him.'

The learned Professor was utterly overwhelmed when his warlike kinsman announced his purpose, in language which implied no doubt of its being a proposal which would be, and ought to be, accepted with the utmost gratitude.

But he feared the plan would put his boy on the road to the gallows. The Professor pleaded that the lad was very young, and in an infirm state of health, and not yet able to endure the hardships of a mountain life; but that in another year or two he hoped his health would be firmly established, and he would be in a fitting condition to attend on his brave kinsman, and follow out the splendid destinies to which he opened the way.

This agreement being made, the cousins parted - Rob Roy pledging his honour to carry his young relation to the hills with him on his next return to Aberdeenshire, and Dr. Gregory, doubtless, praying in his secret soul that he might never see Rob's Highland face again.

James Gregory, who thus escaped being his kinsman's recruit, and in all probability his henchman, was afterwards Professor of Medicine in the College, and, like most of his family, distinguished by his scientific acquirements.

He was rather of an irritable and obstinate disposition; and his friends were wont to remark, when he showed any symptom of these foibles, 'Ah! this comes of not having been educated by Rob Roy'.

The connection between Rob Roy and his classical kinsman did not end with the period of Rob's transient power.

At a period considerably subsequent to the year 1715, he was walking in the Castle Street of Aberdeen, arm-in-arm with his host, Dr. James Gregory, when the drums in the barracks suddenly beat to arms, and soldiers were seen issuing from the barracks.

'If these lads are turning out,' said Rob, taking leave of his cousin with great composure, 'it is time for me to look after my safety.' So saying, he dived down a close, and as John Bunyan says, 'went upon his way and was seen no more'.

We have already stated that Rob Roy's conduct during the insurrection of 1715 was very equivocal. His person and followers were in the Highland army, but his heart seems to have been with the Duke of Argyll's.

Yet the insurgents were constrained to trust to him as their only guide, when they marched from Perth towards Dunblane, with the view of crossing the Forth at what are called the Fords of Frew.

This movement to the westward, on the part of the insurgents, brought on the battle of Sheriff-muir - indecisive, indeed, in its immediate results, but of which the Duke of Argyll reaped the whole advantage.

In this action, it will be recollected that the right wing of the Highlanders broke and cut to pieces Argyll's left wing, while the clans on the left of Mar's army, though consisting of Stewarts, Mackenzies, and Camerons, were completely routed.

During this medley of flight and pursuit, Rob Roy retained his station on a hill in the centre of the Highland position; and though it is said his attack might have decided the day he could not be prevailed upon to charge.

This was the more unfortunate for the insurgents, as the leading of a party of the Macphersons had been committed to MacGregor.

This, it is said, was owing to the age and infirmity of the chief of that name, who, unable to lead his clan in person, objected to his heir-apparent, Macpherson of Nord, discharging his duty on that occasion; so that the tribe, or a part of them, were brigaded with their allies, the MacGregors.

One of the Macphersons, named Alexander, a cattle drover by trade, was so incensed at the inactivity of his temporary leader, that he threw off his plaid, drew his sword, and called out to his clansmen, 'Let us endure this no longer! If he will not lead you, I will.'

Rob Roy replied with great coolness, 'Were the question about driving Highland cows, Sandie, I would yield to your superior skill; but as it respects the leading of men, I must be allowed to be the better judge.'

In the confusion of an undecided field of battle, he enriched his followers by plundering the baggage and the dead on both sides.

The fine old satirical ballad on the battle of Sheriff-muir does not forget to stigmatise our hero's conduct on this memorable occasion:

'Rob Roy he stood watch
On a hill for to catch
The booty, for aught that I saw, man:
For he ne'er advanced
From the place where he stanced,
Till nae mair was to do there at a', man.'

Notwithstanding the sort of neutrality which Rob Roy had continued to observe during the progress of the Rebellion, he did not escape some of its penalties.

He was included in the act of attainder, and the house in Breadalbane, which was his place of retreat, was burned by General Lord Cadogan, when, after the conclusion of the insurrection, he marched through the Highlands to disarm and punish the offending clans.

But upon going to Inveraray with about forty or fifty of his followers, Rob obtained favour by an apparent surrender of their arms to Colonel Patrick Campbell of Finniah, who furnished them and their leader with protections under his hand.

After the collapse of the rebellion, Rob Roy established his residence at Craig-Royston, near Loch Lomond, in the midst of his own kinsmen, and lost no time in resuming his private quarrel with the Duke of Montrose.

For this purpose he soon got on foot as many men, and well armed too, as he had yet commanded. He never stirred without a bodyguard of ten or twelve picked followers, and without much effort could increase them to fifty or sixty.

The Duke was not wanting in efforts to destroy this troublesome adversary. His Grace applied to General Carpenter, commanding the forces in Scotland, and by his orders three parties of soldiers were directed from the three different points of Glasgow, Stirling, and Finlarig near Killin.

Mr Graham of Killearn, the Duke of Montrose's relation and factor, Sheriff-deputy also of Dumbartonshire, accompanied the troops, that they might act under the civil authority, and have the assistance of a trusty guide well acquainted with the hills.

It was the objective of these several columns to arrive about the same time in the neighbourhood of Rob Roy's residence, and surprise him and his followers.

But heavy rain, the difficulties of the country, and the good intelligence which the outlaw was always supplied with, disappointed their well-concerted combination.

The troops, finding the birds were flown, avenged themselves by destroying the nest.

They burned Rob Roy's house, though not with impunity: for the MacGregors, concealed among the thickets and cliffs, fired on them, and killed a grenadier.

Rob Roy avenged himself for the loss which he sustained on this occasion by an act of singular audacity. About the middle of November 1716, John Graham of Killearn, already mentioned as factor of the Montrose family, went to a place called Chapel Errock, where the tenants of the Duke were summoned to appear with their termly rents.

They appeared accordingly, and the factor had received ready money to the amount of about £300, when Rob entered the room at the head of an armed party.

The steward endeavoured to protect the Duke's property by throwing the books of accounts and money into a garret, trusting they might escape notice.

But the experienced freebooter was not to be baffled where such a prize was at stake.

He recovered the books and cash, placed himself calmly in the receipt of customs, examined the accounts, pocketed the money, and gave receipts on the Duke's part, saying he would hold reckoning with the Duke of Montrose out of the damages which he had sustained by his Grace's means, in which he included the losses he had suffered, as well by the burning of his house by General Cadogan, as by the later expedition against Craig-Royston.

He then requested Mr Graham to attend him; nor does it appear that he treated him with any personal violence, or even rudeness, although he informed him he regarded him as a hostage.

Rob removed Graham to an island on Loch Katrine, and caused him to write to the Duke, to state that his ransom was fixed at 3400 merks, being

The MacGregors, concealed among the thickets, fired on them and killed a grenadier

the balance which MacGregor pretended remained due to him, after deducting all that he owed to the Duke of Montrose.

However, after detaining Mr. Graham five or six days in custody on the island, which is still called Rob Roy's prison, and could be no comfortable dwelling for November nights, the outlaw seems to have despaired of attaining further advantage from his bold attempt, and suffered his prisoner to depart uninjured, with the account books and bills granted by the tenants, taking especial care to retain the cash.

About 1717 our chieftain had the dangerous adventure of falling into the hands of the Duke of Athole, almost as much his enemy as the Duke of Montrose himself: but his cunning and dexterity again freed him from certain death.

(The following extract is from a letter which passed from one clergy-man of the Church of Scotland to another, giving some particulars of this escape of Rob Roy, and is taken from an appendix to the novel.)

'My accounts of Rob Roy his escape are yet after severall Embassies between his Grace (who I hear did Correspond with some at Court about it) and Rob he at length upon promise of protection Came to waite upon the Duke & being presently secured his Grace sent post to Edr to acquent the Court of his being apprehended & call his friends at Edr and to desire a party from Gen Carpinter to receive and bring him to Edr which party came the length of Kenross in Fife, he was to be delivered to them by a party his Grace had demanded from the Governor at Perth, who when upon their march towards Dunkell to receive him, were mete with and returned by his Grace having resolved to deliver him by a party of his own men and left Rob at Logierate under a strong guard till ye party should be ready to receive him.

This space of time Rob had Imployed in taking the other dram heartily with the Guard & all were pretty hearty, Rob is delivering a letter for his wife to a servant to whom he must needs deliver some private instructions at the Door (for his wife) where he's attended on the Guard.

When serious in the private Conversatione he is making some few steps carelessly from the Door about the house till he comes by this horse which he soon mounted and made off.

This is no small mortificatio to the guard because of the delay it give to their hopes of a Considerable additional charge against John Roy.'

Other pranks are told of Rob, which argue the same boldness and sagacity as the seizure of Killearn. The Duke of Montrose, weary of his insolence, procured a quantity of arms, and distributed them among his tenantry, in order that they might defend themselves against future attacks.

But they fell into different hands from those they were intended for. The MacGregors made separate attacks on the houses of the tenants, and disarmed them all one after another, not, as was supposed, without the consent of many of the persons so disarmed.

As a great part of the Duke's rents were payable in kind, granaries were established for storing up the corn on the Buchanan estate. To these storehouses Rob Roy used to repair with a sufficient force, and of course when he was least expected, and insist upon the delivery of quantities of grain - sometimes for his own use, and sometimes for the assistance of the country people; always giving regular receipts in his own name, and pretending to reckon with the Duke for what sums he received.

In the meanwhile a garrison was established by the Government half way betwixt Loch Lomond and Loch Katrine, on Rob Roy's original property Inversnaid. Even this military establishment could not bridle the restless MacGregor.

He contrived to surprise the little fort, disarm the soldiers, and destroy the fortification. It was afterwards re-established, and again taken by the MacGregors under Rob Roy's nephew, Ghlune Dhu, previous to the insurrection of 1745-6.

Finally, the fort of Inversnaid was a third time repaired after the extinction of civil discord; and when we find the celebrated General Wolfe commanding in it, the imagination is strongly affected by the variety of time and events which the circumstances brings simultaneously to recollection. It is now totally dismantled.

It was not, strictly speaking, as a professed depredator that Rob Roy now conducted his operations, but as a sort of contractor for the police; in Scottish phrase, a lifter of black-mail.

As the practice of contracting for black-mail was an obvious encouragement to rapine, and a great obstacle to the course of justice, it was, by the statute 1567 chap. 21, declared a capital crime, both on the part of him who levied and him who paid this sort of tax.

But the necessity of the case prevented the execution of this severe law, I believe, in any one instance; and men went on submitting to a certain unlawful imposition, rather than run the risk of utter ruin, just as it is now found difficult or impossible to prevent those who have lost a very large sum of money by robbery from compounding with the felons for restoration of a

part of their booty.

At what rate Rob Roy levied black-mail I never heard stated; but there is a formal contract by which his nephew, in 1741, agreed with various landholders of estates in the counties of Perth, Stirling, and Dumbarton, to recover cattle stolen from them, or to pay the value within six months of the loss being intimated, if such intimation were made to him with sufficient despatch, in consideration of a payment of £5 on each £100 of valued rent, which was not a very heavy insurance.

Petty thefts were not included in the contract; but the theft of one horse, or one head of blackcattle, or of sheep exceeding the number of six, fell under the agreement.

Rob Roy's profits upon such contracts brought him in a considerable revenue in money or cattle, of which he made a popular use; for he was publicly liberal, as well as privately beneficent.

The minister of the parish of Balquhidder, whose name was Robison, was at one time threatening to pursue the parish for an augmentation of his stipend. Rob Roy took an opportunity to assure him that he would do well to abstain from this new exaction, a hint which the minister did not fail to understand.

But to make him some indemnification, MacGregor presented him every year with a cow and a fat sheep; and no scruples as to the mode in which the donor came by them are said to have affected the reverend gentleman's conscience...

It was perhaps about the same time that, by a rapid march into the Balquhidder hills at the head of a body of his own tenantry, the Duke of Montrose actually surprised Rob Roy, and made him prisoner.

He was mounted behind one of the Duke's followers, named James Stewart, and made fast to him by a horse-girth.

It was evening and the Duke was pressing on to lodge his prisoner, so long sought after in vain, in some place of security when, in crossing the Teith or Forth, I forget which, MacGregor took an opportunity to conjure Stewart, by all the ties of old acquaintance and good-neighbourhood, to give him some chance of an escape from an assured doom.

Stewart was moved with compassion, perhaps with fear. He slipped the girth-buckle, and Rob dropping down from behind the horse's croupe, dived, swam, and escaped.

When James Stewart came on shore, the Duke hastily demanded where his prisoner was; and as no distinct answer was returned, instantly suspected Stewart's connivance at the escape of the outlaw, and drawing a steel pistol from his belt struck him down with a blow on the head, from the effects of which, he never completely recovered.

In the success of his repeated escapes from the pursuit of his powerful enemy, Rob Roy at length became wanton and facetious.

He wrote a mock challenge to the Duke, which he circulated among his friends to amuse them over a bottle. It is written in a good hand, and not particularly deficient in grammar or spelling. Our Southern readers must be given to understand that it was a piece of humour, - a quiz, in short - on the part of the outlaw, who was too sagacious to propose such a rencontre in reality. This letter was written in the year 1719.

In the following year Rob Roy composed another epistle, very little to his own reputation, as he therein confesses having played booty during the civil war of 1715.

Rob's fame in the meanwhile passed beyond the narrow limits of the country in which he resided.

A pretended history of him appeared in London during his lifetime, under the title of the *Highland Rogue*. It is a catchpenny publication, bearing in from the effigy of a species of ogre, with beard of a foot in length: and his actions are as much exaggerated as his personal appearance.

Some few of the best known adventures of the hero are told, though with little accuracy: but the greater part of the pamphlet is entirely fictitious.

As Rob Roy advanced in years he became more peaceable in his habits, and his nephew, Ghlune Dhu, with most of his tribe renounced those peculiar quarrels with the Duke of Montrose which his uncle had been distinguished. The policy of that great family had latterly been rather to attach this wild tribe by kindness than to follow the mode of violence.

Leases at a low rent were granted to many of the MacGregors who had heretofore held possessions in the Duke's Highland property merely by occupancy; and Glengyle (or Blackknee), who continued to act as collector of black-mail, managed his police, as commander of the Highland watch arrayed at the charge of Government. He is said to have strictly abstained from the open and lawless depredations which his kinsman had practiced.

It was probably after this state of temporary quiet had been obtained that Rob Roy began to think of the concerns of his future state. He had been bred, and long professed himself a Protestant but in his later years he embraced the Roman Catholic faith - perhaps on Mrs. Cole's principle, that it was a comfortable religion for one of his calling.

In the last year of Rob Roy's life his clan was involved in a dispute with one more powerful than themselves. Stewart of Appin, a chief of the tribe so named, was proprietor of a hill-farm in the Braes of Balquhidder, called Invernenty.

The MacGregors of Rob Roy's tribe claimed a right to it by ancient occupancy, and declared they would oppose to the uttermost the settlement of any person upon the farm not being of their own name. The Stewarts came down with two hundred men, well armed, to do themselves justice by main force. The MacGregors took the field, but were unable to muster an equal strength.

Rob Roy, finding himself the weaker party, asked a parley, in which he represented that both clans were friends to the King, and that he was unwilling they should be weakened by mutual conflict, and thus made a merit of surrendering to Appin the disputed territory of Invernenty.

Appin, accordingly, settled as tenants there, at an easy qui-rent, the MacLarens, a family dependent of the Stewarts, and from whose character for strength and bravery it was expected that they would make their right good if annoyed by the MacGregors.

When all this had been amicably adjusted, in presence of the two clans drawn up in arms near the Kirk of Balquidder, Rob Roy, apparently fearing his tribe might be thought to have conceded too much upon the occasion, stepped forward and said, that where so many gallant men were met in arms, it would be shameful to part without a trial of skill, and therefore he took the freedom to invite any gentleman of the Stewarts present to exchange a few blows with him for the honour of their respective clans.

The brother-in-law of Appin, and second chieftain of the clan, Alaster Stewart of Invernahyle, accepted the challenge, and they encountered with broadsword and target before their respective kinsmen.

The combat lasted till Rob received a slight wound in the arm, which was the usual termination of such a combat when fought for honour only, and not with a mortal purpose.

Rob Roy dropped his point, and congratulated his adversary on having been the first man who ever drew blood from him. The victor generously acknowledged, that without the advantage of youth, and the agility accompanying it, he probably could not have come off with advantage.

This was probably one of Rob Roy's last exploits in arms.

The time of his death is not known with certainty, but he is generally said to have survived 1738, and to have died an aged man.

Alaster Stewart accepted Rob's challenge

When he found himself approaching his final change, he expressed some contrition for particular parts of his life. His wife laughed at these scruples of conscience, and exhorted him to die like a man as he had lived.

In reply, he rebuked her for her violent passions, and the counsels she had given him. 'You have put strife,' he said, 'betwix me and the best men of the country, and now you would place enmity between me and my God.'

There is a tradition, no way inconsistent with the former, if the character of Rob Roy be justly considered, that while on his deathbed he learned that a person with whom he was at enmity proposed to visit him. 'Raise me from my bed,' said the invalid; 'throw my plaid around me, and bring me my claymore, dirk, and pistols - it shall never be said a foeman saw Rob Roy MacGregor defenceless and unarmed.'

His foeman, conjectured to be one of the MacLarens, entered and paid his compliments, inquiring after the health of his formidable neighbour. Rob Roy maintained a cold, haughty civility during their short conference, and so soon as he had left the house, 'Now,' he said, 'all is over - let the piper play *Ha til mi tulidh*' (We return no more): and he is said to have expired before the dirge was finished.

This singular man died in bed in his own house, in the parish of Balquhidder. He was buried in the churchyard of the same parish.

The character of Rob Roy is, of course, a mixed one. His sagacity, boldness, and prudence, qualities so highly necessary to success in war, became in some degree vices, from the manner in which they were employed.

On the other hand, he was in the constant exercise of virtues, the more meritorious as they seem inconsistent with his general character.

Pursuing the occupation of a predatory chieftain - in modern phrase, a captain of banditti - Rob Roy was moderate in his revenge, and humane in his successes.

No charge of cruelty or bloodshed, unless in battle, is brought against his memory.

In like manner, the formidable outlaw was the friend of the poor, and, to the utmost of his ability, the support of the widow and the orphan - kept his word when pledged - and died lamented in his own wild country, where there were hearts thankful for his beneficence, though their minds were not sufficiently instructed to appreciate his errors.

Scottish bestsellers from Lang Syne

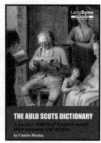

Story of a nation: Scotland
ISBN 1-85217-136-7
£9.99

The Auld Scots Dictionary
ISBN 1-85217-025-5
£10.95

Strange old Scots customs and superstitions
ISBN 0-946264-05-8
£4.99

Scottish Proverbs
ISBN 0-946264-08-2
£4.99

Ghosts, massacres and horror stories of Scotland's castles
ISBN 0-946264-70-8
£4.99

Story of the Saltire
ISBN 1-85217-173-1
£4.99

Prophecies of the Brahan Seer
ISBN 1-85217-136-7
£5.99

Flight of the Midgie
ISBN 1-85217-116-2
£2.99